Surviving the **STRESS** of Your Parents' Old Age

How to Stay Organized, Loving, and Sane

While Caring for Them

by Nan McAdam

Thank You!
For purchasing Surviving the STRESS of Your
Parents' Old Age.

Join our mailing list and get our
complimentary Elder Care Workbook.

Visit us on line to sign up at
http://www.caring4youragingseniorcitizen.com/

If you find this book informative and you enjoy
it, please be kind and review it with kind
words and many stars! Thank you!

DEDICATION

I'm so grateful for my elderly loved ones with whom I have had the opportunity to be an active part in the winter of their lives. I've learned so much about life, myself, and love. Without them, there wouldn't be a book and I wouldn't have grown into the person who I am today.

I'm also grateful for my family, who have encouraged me all along the way. My children make me feel like the luckiest woman on the planet! A special thanks to my husband, Scott, who has been with me every step of the way in our elder care saga.

And finally, to you the reader. If it were not for you, there wouldn't be any reason for this book. My wish for you is to find the answers you are seeking in this book and its references. Giving care to an elder when they are unable to do it themselves is the ultimate in love. It can be frustrating and stressful as heck, but if you allow it, it can change you forever for the better.

TABLE OF CONTENTS

INTRODUCTION

*"Do not resent growing old. Many are denied
the privilege."*

~Author Unknown

It was a bright sunny August day in 1998. My parents and
my thirteen-year-old son had driven to the pioneer cemetery 100 miles away from home to do their usual upkeep.
They were mowing and pruning the cemetery, which held
the graves of many of our relatives from the mid-1800s. It
was a labor of love my parents and my children had been
involved in for many years.

My father began to complain about a dull, excruciating
pain in his mid-back. My dad never complains about anything, much less anything health-related. They decided
to head for home. After loading up the tractors and other
yard equipment, they made their getaway. By the time they
had drawn close to the nearest hospital, Dad was strongly
suggesting a stop at the Emergency Room. Upon arrival
there, they discovered Dad was the unwilling participant
in a major cardiac event. He received the first helicopter
ride of his life... for his life.

Little did I know, on that hot August day, I would be starting a new chapter in my life – the chapter known as elder
care. I was naïve. I didn't know the first thing about taking

care of anyone in the winter of their life. As I began my sometimes stressful, sometimes joyful odyssey, I made many mistakes. I spent many hours researching topics of elder care, trying to make a difference in my parents' new life of sometimes stifling dependence on me.

I felt completely unprepared for this journey. I didn't have any experience in medicine, much less in geriatric care. Each day brought a need for a different set of skills I hadn't mastered. I felt unprepared to handle many things, such as the role reversal that comes with a child becoming the caregiver of a parent. This was only one of the things that took me by surprise.

I was confused as to where to go for information. The world of elder care is huge! As the Internet became a bigger presence in my life, I found information scattered all through cyberspace and beyond. Most of the information I found on the Internet was from well- meaning professionals. I was desperately in need of real life examples and explanations. I became a master of uncovering helpful info from all kinds of different sources.

Time marched on and Dad began to show signs of dementia. In the meantime, Mom's behavior became more demanding, and often abusive. Because of my lack of experience, I was slow to realize she was starting down the road of lost memories called Alzheimer's.

My life became more and more stressful. I was dealing with increased demands on my time, taking me away from my career. I was balancing my family, my job, and my life, with the rapidly escalating demands of elder care. I was locked in to a new school of hard knocks, with so much riding on it and on me. I realized I wasn't alone in my stressful life or in my classroom of elder care. More and more people are stuck in this sandwich generation of care giving. We are caring for our children or grandchildren and our parents. How did this all happen?

Growing old... what strides we have taken in the past 50 years! People are living longer and, for the most part, are in better shape as they age. Our society has made great advances in geriatric medicine and wellness.

Average life expectancy has risen because of these advances. The life expectancy of a male living in the USA is 75.7 years, and for a female it is 80.8 years. Many are finding out that old age has its advantages and disadvantages.

Our society has conquered many diseases which ravaged the population of generations past. Without modern medicine and "wonder drugs," infections and diseases took their toll. As a result of the many medical discoveries, people are living longer, and age-related diseases are on the rise! Dementia, Alzheimer's, and diabetes, just to name a few, are prevalent in our elderly.

Even as our lifestyle changes and our medical advances have marched on, our society has changed. In past generations, it was common for the elderly to live with the extended family unit. Their children and grandchildren provided for their care. Today, most of our elderly population lives separately from their children and grandchildren.

Many older people choose to move to a community of their peers. My parents didn't want to move from their home. Because of their desire to stay in their home and maintain their independence, this became my goal. Not only did I want to keep them in their home, but I needed to do it safely, for as long as possible.

My parents were able to live in their own home until my father was 88 years old and my mother was 83. What a blessing for them! A blessing which came wrapped in hard work and a large amount of stress for my family and me.

My husband and I have not only taken care of my mom and dad, but we have dealt with the illnesses and deaths of my father-in-law and my stepfather-in-law. We have also been caring for two dear friends, whose only sons passed before our friends needed elder care, leaving them in the devastating and heart-wrenching situation of having no family to care for them. They needed surrogate children to make the care decisions for them. My husband and I stepped in. We have spent many hours receiving our "elder care" degree from that University of Hard Knocks, better known as the seat of our pants.

Unlike our unfortunate friends whose sons have passed and who have no family to care for them, I have been blessed to have loving support in my own immediate family. I also have a wonderful and supportive family on my husband's side. For instance, I love my mother-in-law. She is a second mother to me, and one of my best friends. She is going to appear often in this book; I'm going to refer to her as Mom2.

Mom2 is now at the age where she is beginning to need to use our vast amount of knowledge to help her live independently for as long as possible. As I am writing this book, she has gone through a double mastectomy for breast cancer and survived several extended hospital stays for congestive heart failure.

Some of the things that can derail our ability to provide quality care to our elderly loved ones are: the lack of knowledge, the feelings of isolation, and the overwhelming stress of constant care with no known time frame of completion. This book is intended to help readers on the path of elder care find knowledge, solace, and tactics to enrich your experience. My goal in writing this book is to pass down the information I have learned, thus helping others find their own way in the world of elder care and senior living.

My advice for you in your journey with elder care, is to undertake this experience with all the love and patience you can muster. It isn't an easy project. It is fraught with stresses you probably didn't even know were possible.

There will be many times when you feel like you could pull out your hair from frustration or lose it in mass quantities from the stress. That's understandable. It is my hope that there will also be times when you'll have the satisfaction of knowing that what you are doing for them makes a positive difference in their lives!

During my odyssey of elder care, I try to keep in mind how much it matters to them. I remind myself of all the times they were there for me. They bestowed love upon me when

I was growing up and needed them. They would have moved mountains to do the same for me.

Love isn't something we can put in a box and label. It has so many faces. I choose to show the love on my face and in my actions as much as possible when I am with them. Do I get annoyed, short tempered, and completely stressed out sometimes? Yes, absolutely. Those are the times I walk away to regroup and come back refreshed.

Showing them our loving face is a choice we can make every day. It's like happiness. Happiness isn't something you find like a shiny shell on the beach. It's a practice we can choose to follow. It is my hope that the personal stories and information in this book will help you in your own adventures in elder care. So, let's get started.

LOOK WHO'S TAKING CARE OF MOM!

*"There are two ways of spreading light -- to
be the candle or the mirror that reflects it."*

~Edith Wharton

When I look back on my twenties and thirties, I would never have imagined I would be caring for a generation of my older loved ones. Back then, they were in my current role. They were taking care of their elderly loved ones.

Our lives flow like an ever turning wheel. As our life wheel revolves, either suddenly or gradually, we change places with our parents. As children, we are the care receivers and they are providing for our physical and emotional needs. When they age, it becomes harder and harder for them to care for themselves and we become the caregivers.

Care giving doesn't wear just one suit of clothes. There are two distinct types of care giving: the professional caregiver and the informal caregiver.

THE PROFESSIONAL CAREGIVER

The professional caregivers are doctors, Physician's Assistants, nurses, aides, social workers, adult day care workers, or anyone else who gets paid a wage for the job of caring for the elderly.

People successful in the field of care giving for the elderly are unique people. The best professional caregivers have a special personality. They enjoy dealing with older people who have different needs. It takes compassion and caring to sit and listen to elderly people.

Older people are often cut off from others and can be lonely. When they go to their doctor's appointments they like to talk and talk. It takes a loving and compassionate person to sit and listen, then gracefully move them back to the topic at hand, staying vigilant to find out what is really going on in their elderly patient's life.

A perfect example of this was when Mom2 and I were at the surgeon's office for a post-mastectomy check. One of the things I enjoy about this particular doctor is his great sense of humor. He likes to laugh and tease a little. Mom2 thinks the world of him.

He is a very busy surgeon, but he always stops and listens to what she has to say. Mom2 has balance issues. She will topple over all of a sudden. She gets dizzy, but doesn't pass out. She had one of her little episodes while she was in the waiting room. She didn't fall all the way down, because I was standing close enough to her and she fell into me.

While she was having her check, she mentioned that she was clumsy. I could tell by watching him, his ears perked up. He was smiling as he asked her if she had become "clumsy" since the operation or was she that way before.

She explained her problem, with a little input from me.

He was concerned. He told her how dangerous falls are for anyone, but especially for her since she is diabetic and on a blood thinner. He explained that she needs to use her walker. She always resists using a walker; she doesn't want to appear "old."

She is very strong willed and knows her own mind. It takes a lot to change her mind once it is made up. They playfully argued for a short time, but he finally got his message across.

The doctor is the head of the Trauma department for one of the largest hospitals in our city. He told her about a lady who was the same age as Mom2 with similar medical issues. She had fallen the week before, hit her head, and had begun to bleed into her brain. Even after doing surgery, they couldn't get the bleeding to stop, and she had passed away.

This story helped Mom2 understand the dangers of falling and hitting her head. He's very good at reading his patients. He was able to get his message across to her because he has always treated her with respect, love, and a saucy dose of humor. Mom2 always responds well to humor... especially with a little zing to it! She enjoys a good laugh and likes being around others who do.

He made her promise to use her walker. He was an effective closer by having her verbally promise him she would use it. He didn't just warn her and let it drop; he asked her for her word, over and over again, until he got it. If he didn't care, he would have mentioned using her walker, and moved on to another topic.

Effective elder care professionals are people who prefer taking care of others. They enjoy putting other people's needs first. They find satisfaction in supporting and aiding those less fortunate, or the elderly. They respect those who have been seasoned with experience and, because of declining health, need more help.

Good caregivers are good listeners, like Mom2's surgeon. They care to hear what is going on in their patients' lives. Their listening skills have to be above the norm. They are invested in their patients' lives. They are usually very busy people, because of their extraordinary skill with this age group. When they are with their patient, the patient is the only person on the planet. They listen attentively, knowing it can help give them a fuller picture of what their patient is experiencing. This skill helps them improve the accuracy of any diagnosis.

A great caregiver won't take it personally, get upset or ruffled, or attempt to "get even" with a patient whose mood isn't pleasant. They understand that moods can turn nasty when a patient doesn't feel well or is frustrated by their circumstances. They show amazing amounts of patience with the elderly. They don't react adversely when their elderly patient is hurting and scared and misbehaves.

It is important to pick a good caregiver. In the case of a doctor, they can be the difference between living and dying. My family found out the hard way about picking the wrong type of person for an elder care doctor.

Over ten years ago, Dad had a stroke. He was rushed to the hospital in an ambulance. After examining him, his doctor said he had a brain stem stroke. In the doctor's eyes, he was as good as dead.

Dad had a living will. A DNR (Do Not Resuscitate) order was placed on his chart. Then the neurologist came in to visit. He explained that because of Dad's constant erratic movements, it was impossible to do an MRI on him. The neurologist believed Dad could recover from this stroke. This left us, the family, in a quandary. Whom do we believe?

As a family, we prayed about it. Our prayers were answered by Dad's going into cardiac arrest. The hospital staff wasn't going to do anything about it. Mom, being a quick decision maker, overrode the DNR status. Attendants then rushed in with the crash cart, used the defibrillator paddles on him, and stabilized him. His doctor wasn't pleased about this, but Mom had the power. She believed Dad would get better; her intuition told her so. She was a strong advocate for him.

Dad's doctor still believed he would die. He took him off all fluids. It was heartbreaking to watch Dad suffering from dehydration. The symptoms of late stage dehydration are too awful to list. Mom and I didn't believe Dad's internist was correct. We decided to seek a second opinion.

My husband contacted his brother, who was a paramedic, and asked him what doctor was especially good with geriatric patients. He knew right away who fit the bill and we contacted his suggested doctor. We were able to set him up to see Dad.

In the meantime, Dad was showing improvement in spite of the dehydration. Dad's doctor wouldn't accept the improvements as indications Dad was getting better. The doctor had a huge argument with Mom in the hallway outside Dad's room. He was nasty and yelled at her, "Face it, your husband's going to die!" Mom, being a no-nonsense gal, told him, "You're fired!"

The other doctor came in and put him back on fluids. Within a couple of hours, Dad was sitting up in bed talking to all of us. Dad kept asking my youngest son to go get him a Pepsi. The orders on his chart called for no liquids by mouth due to swallowing issues. My poor conflicted son kept saying, "Grandpa, I can't get you a Pepsi!"

After three or four requests Mom said, "Drew, if your Grandpa wants a Pepsi, go get him one!" Dad swigged that can of Pepsi down in one long drink, followed by the world's longest burp! The sugar revitalized him. He continued to improve and we had him out of the hospital in less than a week after his resurrection with the help of a can of Pepsi.

My point with this story is not to sell Pepsi. It is to illustrate how important it is to have the right professional caregiver. Dad had gone to the original doctor for over fifteen years. The doctor was so absorbed in what he believed was Dad's prognosis, he wouldn't listen to the advice of the neurologist. This doctor was bound and determined Dad was going to die! His treatment of the family was inexcusable.

My intuition had been telling me for a while that this doctor wasn't the best one for Dad. Dad was unwilling to change and I didn't trust my intuition enough to make a stand against the doctor. Who would have thought he would behave like that? Older patients get used to a certain doctor and they don't want to change. But if your gut is telling you something is not right with a professional caregiver, honor those feelings. Because I didn't honor my gut instincts, Dad lives with compromised kidneys, a leftover from the drastic dehydration.

A good professional caregiver has good advice. They have been around for a while and have seen many different things. This experience, added to their caring nature, makes them a good source of advice and information. I have met so many loving and caring professional care givers in my career of elder care. I have appreciated their loving advice more than I can express.

I've had many opportunities to see professionals who are great caregivers, and those who aren't. If you are concerned about the care your elder is receiving, or the professional seems to lack the special skills to deal with them, don't be afraid to change to someone else. It is much easier to work with a loving elder care professional.

THE INFORMAL CAREGIVER

If there is ever a question about the goodness of mankind, go look for an informal caregiver. I am amazed by the depth of their love. Giving care to anyone who has physical or mental issues is challenging.

When we grow older, we can change places with our parents. We can suddenly find ourselves in the role of caring for them. The roles are reversed, and the child becomes the parent. This can make it a bumpy road.

If you are starting on your journey of providing care for someone, you are not alone. According to the Family Caregiver Alliance which is the National Center on Caregiving, "Twenty-five to thirty-five percent of the workforce is providing elder care in some form or another. Nearly half of caregivers provide fewer than eight hours of care per week, while nearly one in five provide more than 40 hours of care per week. For dementia patients, this can be even higher.

"The duration of care giving can last from less than a year to more than 40 years. The study conducted in 2003 found that caregivers provided care for an average of 4.3 years."

Caregivers come in all colors, shapes, and sizes. They can be caring friends, neighbors, spouses, and adult children. Caregivers can bring the elder into their home. They can provide care in the elder's home. There isn't one pattern where "one size fits all."

In the case of my parents, they were able to live in their home with certain services coming in. It was only when it became unsafe for them to live independently, due to the effects of dementia, that we were forced to seek an alternative living situation.

Giving care to an elderly loved one can be very stressful. They fall down, need extra help with everyday living, and have mental and physical issues to deal with. There are numerous doctor visits and hospital stays.

Many times, the caregiver has stress-related issues they have to deal with in their own life. "Studies have found that caregivers may have increased blood pressure and insulin levels. They may experience impaired immune systems and increased risk for cardiovascular disease among other adverse health outcomes. In the case of a spouse, the spouse's physical condition can deteriorate faster than that of the loved one they are caring for.

Depression is the most common among informal caregivers with 20% to 50% reporting depressive disorders or symptoms. The highest level of depression is reported by those caregivers who are taking care of dementia patients."

As dismal as those facts may be, I would be misinforming you if I paint only a bleak picture of informal care giving. It can be a rewarding and satisfying pursuit. Being able to have such a dramatic effect on another person by caring for them can be gratifying. It can depend on how the caregiver perceives it. It is also much easier if the elder is appreciative of the efforts being made. But, sadly, that is not always the case.

Often, when our older person isn't feeling well, or is frightened by the many changes taking place in their life, they can strike out at their caregiver. If they start having symptoms of dementia, their personality can change. For instance, the happy older person can become uncharacteristically grouchy and contrary.

I have read many inspiring stories of loved ones caring for their elders until they pass. It forms a relationship beyond all others. It is a special bond of love we can only share with those we care for.

I highly recommend you line up all the emotional support you can. There are support groups who are just a mouse click away on the Internet. There are many informal caregivers who are making the same journey as you. These amazing people can be found in elder care forums on the Internet. Visit a few, and join at least one. Get to know these loving people. I have been deeply moved by the sharing on these sites. There are also some wonderful tips you can discover from others who are seasoned veterans. It is rewarding to be able to share what you know, and help others.

Check with professional caregivers and see if they know of any groups meeting, of people in the same situation. Social Workers are a great source of information and support.

I have been fortunate to have a family support system that has always lifted me up and helped me go on for another day.

Elder care is stressful! Realize it and do something to refill your soul. Take time out for yourself. If you are in a 24/7 situation with your elder care, it is very important to find someone who can step in for you. This gives you an opportunity to take a break, and do something you enjoy doing. This helps you relax and unwind. It is vitally important to keep our own emotional cups filled while we care for others.

WHEN IS SNOOPING GOOD?

"I feel the capacity to care is the thing which
gives life its deepest significance."

~ Pablo Casals

Every piece of flesh on this Earth appreciates their privacy to different degrees. When we grow up in a family, we're aware of this. Maybe we've even copied it in our own lives.

Sooner or later, if we are lucky, we will live long enough that we might need help in our everyday world. When our parents get to that stage, is our first thought "they won't appreciate my meddling in their affairs"? We may feel like we are snooping in their lives. How can we tell when it's time to get involved and take a more proactive stance in our elder's life?

This is a time when communication is paramount. It doesn't usually go well to barge in and start taking over. I've seen it happen. It can cause so many hard feelings.

SHOULD I GET INVOLVED?

Many years ago, I was talking with my husband's grandma. She was born in 1900 and lived to be 92 years old. I loved hearing the stories about yesteryear, which were still so fresh in her mind.

She was born in a time when most people traveled by horse and buggy. During her lifetime, transportation took some unbelievable jumps! People went from horse and buggies to the automobile. The Wright brothers flew their first flight at Kitty Hawk, North Carolina on December 17, 1903. She witnessed many wars, space flight, and a man walking on the moon.

With the invention of the airplane, the world became a smaller place. Many people have moved many miles away from their parents' home. A visit home to Mom and Dad's might happen only once or twice a year. Being so far away from parents can make it hard to get involved in their everyday lives. But it is easier to recognize a decline in their health when the visits are infrequent.

As I mentioned before, I live in the same town as my parents. It was harder to recognize the day-to-day decline of their health. For me, their declining health was punctuated by hospital stays and episodes of emergency visits.

My Dad loved to sit in a hot bath and steam his troubles away. The first time he got stuck in the tub and was too weak to get out, my husband went over and had the strength to lift him out. That "silly" inconvenience didn't stop Dad from his ritual bath.

The second time, we were out of town on a business trip, and the neighbor next door had to be summoned by Mom to help him. The third time, it was the fire department.

They had a two-bathroom home, so at that point we disabled his tub; we purchased a shower assist chair, and then found a professional caregiver to give him some assistance in bathing.

Dad is a veteran of WWII. His veteran status has been a lifesaver for him. My parents live on a small fixed income of Social Security and a small VA pension.

He started going to the Veterans Hospital for physicals and medications after he retired. When he began to have his episodes in the tub, I contacted the VA and set up bathing services for him. They also provided some light housekeeping help for my mother.

As I said before, when you live a distance from your parents and only see them a few times a year, the changes they are going through are more obvious. But even living in town, I started noticing changes in my parents.

Here's a list of some of the things to watch for:

1. Are they bathed and well groomed?
2. Hair cut, washed and styled?
3. Fingernails clean?
4. Teeth brushed and breath smelling good?
5. Their clothes well-maintained and clean or are they dirty, stained, or ripped?
6. Are they wearing the same clothes too many days in a row?
7. Are their clothes fitting properly?
8. Have they had an unusual change in weight – gained or lost?

9. Are they eating healthy meals or have their eating habits changed?
10. Are they having trouble hearing or seeing well?
11. Do they seem more lethargic than usual?
12. Are they moving around as well as before?
13. Is their gait regular?
14. Are they weak or unbalanced?
15. Different stages of bruising and scratches that could mean frequent falls or abuse.
16. Are they holding on to furniture or walls as they move around their home?
17. How are they sleeping?
18. Have their sleep habits changed?
19. Are they sleeping more or less than in previous years?
20. Do they have bruised or swollen legs, ankles, or feet?
21. Do they need help dressing, bathing, or using the toilet?
22. Are they taking their medicines as prescribed?
23. Do they understand the dosages and when to take them?
24. Do they have extra pills left over at the end of the month?
25. Are they needing refills on prescriptions before they should?
26. Are they missing appointments?
27. Are they acting like themselves?
28. Are they repeating stories or questions?
29. Are they more forgetful than usual?
30. Are they crying or getting angry more easily?

31. Are they fearful of things that didn't worry them before?
32. Have they lost interest in activities and/or hobbies they used to enjoy?
33. Are they staying home more and limiting social engagements?
34. Are they drinking alcoholic beverages more often?
35. How is their driving? Have them drive for you.
36. Are their reflexes slower?
37. Have they gotten lost going to familiar places?
38. Have they stopped driving at night?
39. Are there new dents or dings on the car or garage?
40. Do they know where the car or garage damage came from?
41. Has their housekeeping declined? Does the house smell clean?
42. Are their linens clean?
43. Has home maintenance declined or stopped?
44. Is yard work done?
45. Are pets and/or house plants being taken care of adequately?
46. Is the food old or expired? Check dates on milk, cottage cheese, etc.
47. Are the refrigerator, pantry, counter tops, and cupboards clean?
48. Is food that should be refrigerated getting left out on the counter?
49. Is the house cluttered? Are the garbage and trash being taken out regularly?
50. Is the mail piling up and not being opened?
51. Bills lost or not paid?

52. Are the newspapers being read and discarded in a timely manner?
53. Unsafe situations such as hair dryers and other appliances near sinks, tubs, and other water sources?
54. Using power tools outside or near hazards?
55. Wearing inappropriate clothing for the weather conditions?
56. Are pathways strewn with things to trip them such as electrical cords and rugs?

Our parents are as unique as snowflakes. Not all of these things fit our particular situations. Using this list can help us to stay vigilant in watching for signs that we need to step in and help them. But sometimes we will have to go on our gut feelings in these areas.

When we watch for the little signs that our loved one needs some help, we may be able to avoid situations such as getting stuck in the tub, or falling and being unable to get up.

IS IT TIME TO GO TO THE DOCTOR WITH THEM?

My philosophy has always been: *I don't want to take away from them things they are still able to do; that creates a dependence on me. Soon, they become unable to do them at all. Every time I take over something, it erodes their self-esteem regarding their ability to take care of themselves.* You may or may not agree with me. But it has served me well. Remember those snowflakes!

So, if my philosophy is true, how can we tell they need our help at the doctor's office? One of the first signs to watch for in this area is when they can't remember what was said or what happened at the doctor's office. Often both parents would go together to appointments. This was very helpful, when one of them could remember what was said, or the changes in medications.

Before I started accompanying them to the doctor's, I would always ask what the doctor had said. To me, it was evident when I needed to step in and accompany them. We talked about it and they were relieved to know I would go with them. At that time, I didn't have knowledge or experience with elder care. I had to rely on my gut feelings in this area.

I believe this is one of the first areas where we should begin helping our elders. It's helpful to have a second pair of ears to hear what the doctor has to say. I've kept a little notebook in my purse or pocket that is dedicated to their health care. I write myself notes in it when I notice something to ask the doctor about. I write notes at the doctor's office when they are discussing my loved one's health. It keeps it fresh in my mind when they have forgotten or question something; it is easy to refer back to my little notebook! It works like a mini journal. I have multiple seniors to care for, so I have to be very organized in my little book. Their name, date, and doctor we are visiting is at the top of the page. This tip has served me well.

Another sign to watch for is missed or forgotten appointments. I suggest, even before you become involved in their health care, that you have your name listed on their doctors' records as the person who can receive information on their health care. The current privacy policies and laws are very stringent. If you are not listed on their records, you will not get information from their doctors or their offices.

DEALING WITH MEDICATIONS

A crucial time to help our senior is when they start having difficulty with their medications. Mom was having trouble with their medicines. She was filling both Dad's pill box and her own. I could tell she was frustrated and I simply asked if I could help. She was relieved to turn it over to me.

Eventually, it became increasingly difficult for Mom to take her own medications. She became very combative with me, blaming me for the inaccuracies of her pill boxes. At the end of the week, she either had too many pills left or not enough. I saw this as a sign that she was either over-medicating or under-medicating. Either way, her medication wasn't being taken as directed.

On one of our many visits to the doctor, I relayed what I felt was going on. I was able to get the doctor to give us a referral for help with the pill boxes. When a referral is given by the doctor, Medicare usually will pay for the service. I was able to bring in a nursing company to come in and do this for her. This relieved some of the stress and friction between Mom and me.

The Veterans Administration started sending in a home nurse to fill Dad's pill box at about the same time. I learned from all of this, to keep communicating with the different agencies. For me, the Veterans Administration has been the easiest to deal with. Here in Iowa, which is all I can speak for, the Veterans Administration loves their vets and takes very good care of them.

Once Dad had an in-home social worker from the VA on his case, communicating got easier. The Veterans Administration has a book available that outlines all their services. The book is called FEDERAL BENEFITS FOR VETERANS AND DEPENDENTS. It is put out by the Department of Veterans Affairs.

Dad's in-home social worker helped us file the paperwork for services. Because of his small monthly income, Dad was able to receive a dramatically reduced cost on his prescriptions.

HOME MAINTENANCE ISSUES

I must take a moment to say I am the luckiest woman alive on this planet! I have a wonderful supportive husband. My parents are older than his. I'm the youngest child and he is the eldest in his family. Perfect combo for us.

Dad loved to mow his yard. It is just a spit of a thing. Most of their yard is cement driveway for a three-car garage setup. Mom, being a woman with a green thumb, enjoyed putting most of their lawn into a garden. This was great, until Mom couldn't take care of it anymore. When it became obvious that Dad couldn't get the mower started and his health had deteriorated to the point he couldn't take care of the mowing and snow removal, my husband jumped right in and took care of it for them.

I'm blessed to have a handy husband. If home maintenance isn't your thing, or your health doesn't allow for you to take over these responsibilities, it may be time to hire it out. This may be difficult if you and your loved one are living on a small fixed income. I found out that in our area of the country we have a very active and reputable Seniors Helping Seniors group. Many retired people with various talents help other senior citizens do things around their homes. There are many things they can help with: electrical, plumbing, roofing, gutters, lawn work, etc. They work for a small fee.

Be aware: there are many unethical people who prey on seniors. They call on the phone or come to the door, offering to paint, put up gutters, etc. They will overcharge or downright steal from unsuspecting senior citizens.

I had to keep an ear always trained on conversations with Mom. She would sometimes fall for these tactics! She has always been a decision maker; Dad is not. In fact, Mom made all the decisions. She wasn't used to running anything by someone else for feedback. Sometimes I found out too late about these experiences. It is always best to know the Better Business Bureau's phone number and make contact with them if you are in doubt about the reputation of a company or individual in business. It's important, if you have had a bad business experience with a company, to report them to the Better Business Bureau in your area. This can help the next person avoid a bad situation.

My parents, living on a very low, fixed income, had a lot of neglected home maintenance. Even with my handy husband, many things were too costly to repair.

Whether it is going to the doctor with them, filling their medication pill boxes, or doing home maintenance, watch for the signs that they are no longer able to do it for themselves. This may happen quickly after an illness, or slowly and gradually from the onset of dementia.

LONE RANGER VS. A HORSE OF A DIFFERENT COLOR

"When we do the best that we can, we never know what miracle is wrought in our life, or in the life of another."

~ Helen Keller

Years ago, taking care of our moms and dads was a different situation. Most families had a maiden sister or aunt who stayed home with the parents and took care of them until they passed. The maiden care giver didn't have another job, and was supported by the family members who married and moved away.

Things have changed dramatically in the culture of the United States. The maiden lady who only has skills as a caregiver and takes care of the parents until they die, has disappeared.

What hasn't disappeared is the fact that one sibling usually ends up doing the majority of the care giving. There are exceptions, where siblings who live close can take turns with the responsibilities of caring for the elder family members. If there is a sharing of responsibilities in your situation, feel blessed. It doesn't often happen that way.

On my side of the family, as I mentioned before, I am the only sibling who chose to stay in the same city with my parents. I am the youngest of four daughters. My siblings are spread across the Midwest. The closest sister, willing to help, is a three-hour drive away.

There are as many family dynamics as there are families. You aren't alone if you have family politics flourishing in your family. Frustrating, I know. When it comes to decisions about Mom and Dad, it seems either everyone is together or no one can agree. Being alone in elder care can feel like we're the Lone Ranger, saddling up our trusty steed, Silver, and riding into the great unknown.

Dealing with our elderly parents can be stressful. There can be a tremendous amount of pressure involved, especially if either parent is suffering from some form of dementia.

There are frequent trips to the hospital, as their health declines. If you have ever waited in a hospital Emergency Room, you know it is a test of patience. The wait is long, even when ER traffic is light. As the population grows and ages, and health care laws change, I don't see a change in this, except to get worse.

When the caregiver has a job outside of the home, frequent hospital visits can mean a loss of income. Some companies are not understanding about time away from work because of care giving responsibilities. No one has a crystal ball, to know how long our loved one may live and need our help. I've felt lucky to have a job where I work from home. I have flexible hours. In other words, I'm self-employed. Being self-employed can seem like a blessing, but it can have a downside, too.

Before Mom's open heart surgery, her heart problems sent her to the Emergency Room often. One admittance clerk referred to her as a "frequent flier." She also made many ambulance trips. I found out that Medicare will not pay for two ambulance trips in one 24-hour period.

In the same time period, Dad almost died. He required several hospital visits in a short period of time.

A week before the Christmas of 2003 found Mom in the hospital. At the same time, a raging flu epidemic in our town was filling the hospitals. The flu shots everyone had taken in the fall of 2003 didn't prevent anyone, including the health care workers, from getting this particular brand of flu.

Dad became ill at the same time and there was no room for him in the hospital. I took him to my home to care for him. My sister, who is an angel to me, and my biggest support, came to town to help. But as fate would have it, she became extremely ill and had to head for home.

With all the pressure from caring for them, loss of income, and many sleepless nights, my health began to suffer. My husband and kids, all of them, had the flu. I kept pushing myself. I figured if the nurses in the hospital could work with the flu, I could keep going.

I usually think of myself as a pretty laid-back individual, but I was one stressed-out lady! I finally crashed and burned on Christmas Eve. I had gotten Mom out of the hospital, and Dad was well enough to return to their house. I couldn't go on anymore.

With my case of the flu, I received an extra dividend of developing cardiomyopathy; the flu had weakened the left ventricle of my heart. The pumping function of my heart, which should be between 50% and 60%, was limping along at 35%. It took me twelve months to get my heart function back up to normal. It made me realize that I needed to take care of myself first. Sounds selfish, doesn't it? But is it really?

Have you ever taken a flight on an airline? If you have, you are very familiar with the speech every passenger gets from the flight staff. The Flight Attendant covers all the rules of airplane safety before takeoff. One of the first things they show us is how to apply our oxygen mask. They explain that we should always put our own oxygen mask on first before we help the children or the elderly with their masks. Why? Isn't it our first instinct to take care of the children and the less able, first? The reason is, if we don't put our mask on first, we could be trying to help the child and lose consciousness in the process. Both will die, because we didn't take care of ourselves first. If we become overwhelmed and stressed out, isn't it the same as the oxygen mask? If we become disabled because of the stress, what good are we to our elderly loved one?

Not only did I stretch myself too thin and become ill while taking care of others, I lost time with my profession. I suffered loss of income. I also incurred extra expenses such as gas, more meals away from home, and a lot of little expenses that eventually added up. Put all of this together, Christmas 2003 wasn't the best one of my life!

What I did get out of all this is, I had to learn, the hard way, to take breaks. I had to learn to let my family, or other helpful people, do some of the things I was doing. I needed to arrange things so I could take weekends away with my husband, to depressurize my life.

I needed to reduce the stress, or I wasn't going to be able to help myself or my parents. I had to learn to take the oxygen mask dangling from the ceiling, and put it on myself first.

With the doctor's and social worker's help, I found services I could bring in to help with my parents. I discovered that the doctor and other professional caregivers were my allies. The professional caregivers understand the stress involved in taking care of our beloved older people.

My suggestion is to talk with your elder's doctor about the stress. Geriatric specialists are very knowledgeable about the services available and the Medicare laws. They can help you find the services to take the load off of you. To qualify for Medicare to pick up some or all of the costs of these in-home services, you will need a referral from the doctor.

COMMUNICATING WITH FAMILY

Many families have what the boss with no eyes said in Cool Hand Luke: "What we have here is a failure to communicate!" Communicating with our families can be such a frustrating area. When my family started the odyssey of taking care of our parents, we weren't all on the same page. One of my sisters didn't want to know or be kept informed about what was going on with our parental units. She was more into sticking her head in the sand and hoping it would all go away. Don't get me wrong, sister #1 is a loving and caring individual. She has her plate full at home. She wanted me to handle it and she was usually supportive of how I cared for our parents. She just didn't want to know what was going on.

Sister #2 wanted my parents to go to assisted living or skilled care, fifteen years before they finally ended up going. She understood my parents' wishes and my goal of keeping them in the home. She didn't agree with it, but she was as loving and supportive as she could be. She stayed in contact with me and wanted me to stay in contact with her. The day-to-day business was for me to decide and she would support my choices.

Sister #3 is really my angel sister, and my rock. She lives three hours away, but is always a great sounding board. She came to town so many weekends to be with my parents and take the pressure off of me. I discussed everything with her. She understood the goal of keeping our parents in their home, and supported it with all her heart. I can't imagine going through this without her.

Once again I have to say, I'm very, very lucky to have a supportive partner. My husband has been with me in all of our elder care endeavors. We function as one in all our decisions and choices.

Only you know the dynamics of your family. If you are the sole care giver, pick the people who will help you and support your decisions. Less communication with the ones who aren't helpful or supportive might be the wisest choice to make.

When my parents could no longer stay in their home due to falling issues and dementia, we, as a family, were eventually on the same page. I am so thankful for all of their love and support.

WHITE HORSE SYNDROME

Some families are not on the same page. As sad as it sounds, when dealing with our moms and dads, the disagreements amongst the siblings can start. Once in a while, a family member can honestly think they are doing the right thing for Mom and Dad, but in the end, it undermines the main caregiver.

I have a dear friend whom I have known for over 30 years. We have always kept in close contact, even though she and her family live half a continent away from me.

Her mom and dad and most of her family live in a rural area in our state. Mom and Dad had a large family, and there were other siblings around the area. But, as is often the case, no one seemed to want to do the running around, bill paying, doctor visiting, etc., which goes along with taking care of the parents. Her youngest sister became the caregiver for her mom and dad.

As time went on, the stress got to the youngest sister. It happens with many family caregivers; the stress makes them ill as well. Youngest sis had a near death experience with Hodgkin's disease. She recovered from that only to be stricken with multiple sclerosis. She is a brave woman whom I hold in high esteem.

The older the mom and dad got, the more their health deteriorated. Dad got Alzheimer's and Mom had explosive incontinence issues and became blind from Macular Degeneration. Very messy situation, to say the least. What a poopy deal for youngest sister to deal with on a daily basis.

Staying in their own home became impossible. They moved to an apartment in a nearby larger town. The dad's Alzheimer's progressed. Poor youngest sis. She was raising a family, had a child with special needs, a job, her own health issues, and was taking care of Mom and Dad. Wow, talk about mega stress!

Finally, a place opened up in the local care facility and youngest sister was able to get them placed. The nursing home is very close to their apartment. Dad adjusted just fine. He was an extrovert and enjoyed the attention he got from the nursing home staff. Mom didn't do as well. In fact, she hated it.

When my friend would call her from far away, Mom would complain and tell her that she didn't want to die in a nursing home. She wanted to be in her own place. Feeling bad for her mom, my friend came home to visit and took Mom and Dad out of the nursing home and back to their apartment. She got them settled. Got a few services set up to take care of them, and flew back to her home. Who was left holding the care giving bag again? None other than youngest sis.

Mom was happy, Dad was confused, and youngest sister went back to being overwhelmed. The moral of the story is, if you aren't going to be around to help with the work, don't ride in on the white horse to save them from the big bad nursing home. It shouldn't be only your decision to move them out of the care facility.

I had a long talk with my friend from far away. I explained how I would have felt if it had been me. She understood and felt bad that she had undone what her sister had worked so hard to do. But, it was done.

SENIORS GONE WILD!

"Remember that everyone you meet is afraid of something, loves something, and has lost something."

~ *H. Jackson Brown, Jr.*

No, I'm not talking about drunk senior citizens hooting and yelling while lewdly wagging their tongues at the camera. Old ladies shaking and swinging naked saggy bosoms around as they shift back and forth on their arthritic legs. As picturesque as that may sound, "seniors gone wild" has a different meaning.

Old age can be a magnifier of undesirable personality traits. Dementia can add a whole new dimension to difficult behavior. If the person has been an impatient person, they can become impossible to please. An irritable person can become enraged. A personality trait that could have been overlooked in the past can be pointed right at the caregiver. The caregiver is the one who can become the main focal point of challenging behavior.

As anyone knows who has grown old or watched someone grow old, there are a lot of things that can feel out of control to an elderly person. They could have incontinence issues, chronic pain, friends who pass on, memory problems... the list goes on. Each of these things can rob our elders of the feeling of having any control in their lives. It can set up a feeling of fear about the future and anger with the aging process.

ELDERS LASHING OUT IN ANGER

As my parents were going through all of this, they had periods when they were angry. Angry with the situation and with me. When they were angry, it hurt me. Even though I know the best advice anyone could give me is "don't take it personally," it was difficult. Mom was especially challenging, because she is a strong personality and very controlling.

Let me set the stage for you in regard to my situation. I love my Mom, but she is a difficult person in the best of times. She can go from the kind and loving Earth Mother personality, to a shrieking, angry, abusive person literally seconds later. The line can be so fine, it can be difficult to know what set her off.

All her life she has had undiagnosed mental issues. She would get angry with Dad and threaten to drag him off to counseling. She would use it as a hammer over his head. He is a very private person and this threat would make him toe her line for a while.

The infrequent and short-term attempts at counseling with a psychologist or pastor were shut down when it was suggested that she had mental issues to deal with. Even the attempts by her doctors to give her something for anxiety and depression would eventually break down due to her tendency to self-medicate. She would simply stop taking the medicine. She never felt that anything was her fault. It was always Dad's fault; therefore, she didn't need professional help.

Mom always refers to herself as "an in-your-face kinda gal." Many times, the face she was in was mine. She would lash out in anger over and over again. She was very demanding of my time. She expected me to be with her 24/7/365. The older she got and the more she progressed into Alzheimer's dementia, the more difficult she became to deal with.

Dad developed the self-preservation ability to disappear into himself. When he was around her, he was quiet and withdrawn. He rarely spoke to her about anything because of the fear of retribution. Anything he did or said was used against him in her court of law.

Dad, even though he is a private person, became a more outgoing personality with the progression of his dementia. He would go for walks and have his favorite haunts to stop in and visit. There's a small shopping center close to their house and he would stop in and see his favorite people almost daily. Sometimes he would be gone longer than Mom felt was necessary and she would call the police to bring him home. There was always hell to pay upon his return. It's understandable that she would be worried about him, but her reactions were over the top. She was angry because he didn't talk to her and would talk to everyone else. I've spent hours talking with her about it. I would always tell her that what she focuses on, grows. There was nothing he could say or do right!

Mom has always been a physical person. I began to worry about Dad's safety. It was difficult to know if there was physical abuse going on, because Dad was on blood thinners and he bruised easily and frequently. When I asked him if she ever hit him, he said "no." I asked him if he would tell me if she did and his response was again, "no." As one of her children and knowing her punishment style, I had strong suspicions.

In retrospect, I've wondered if I should have done anything differently. I did let the social worker know of my concerns. Undesirable behavior doesn't always show up in front of strangers. They did watch out for it. There was no documented reason to do anything about it. As it turned out, when my parents went to the nursing home, they roomed together. After a short time, the staff split them up because they witnessed the abuse.

I'm sure that most of you won't have to deal with the same issues I've had to deal with. Yours will be different. When our parents lash out in anger, it might not even be about what they say it is. It helped for me to remember that they were feeling insecure about their future and the changes taking place in their lives. They had to have complete trust in me, and sometimes, for me, that was a heavy burden.

Often they would be angry about nothing. I had to remind myself that they weren't feeling well. Many older people don't react to change very well at all. Many times, the elder turns on the caregiver, especially if it is their child. It becomes abuse of the caregiver. This type of abuse is common with personality disorders. They turn on the adult child who is showing the most love by care giving, because they feel safe doing it. They may not mean to be abusive, but they are frustrated and need to vent about getting old, or their chronic pain, more dependence on their caregiver, etc.

I tried talking to Mom about it. However, that didn't get far. It usually made it worse. I found comfort in prayer. Prayer helped me release the burdens to my God and accept his help. It helped to remind myself not to take it personally. I fell back on my support system and talked it out with them. I had access to a social worker at the Veterans Hospital, who was my dad's in-home social worker. She was a great source of knowledge and support.

One of the few things I tried that worked was taking myself out of the situation for a while. I retreated to my old habit of staying away from Mom for short periods of time. This was met with angry phone calls and hateful speech, but I was able to regroup. Sometimes she would actually appear to appreciate me more when I returned.

I recommend establishing a network of people you can turn to when times are tough or you need help. It is the best way to lower the stress when times are challenging. It's tough. Whether the burden is shouldered by one, or by the whole family, communication can be challenging. It is important to remember, if one person is doing most of the care giving, they need to be supported. Stay off those white horses!

NOT BATHING

A challenging behavior I often hear about from others is the elder's refusal to take showers, wear fresh clothes, and take care of personal hygiene. This can be very frustrating for the caregiver.

Something to consider with this behavior is depression. If depression doesn't seem to be the issue, it could be about control. As people age, they feel they are losing more and more control over their lives. Hygiene, or the lack of it, can be an issue where they can maintain the feeling of control.

Diminished senses can add to this. Their eyesight gets worse; they don't see the food spots on their clothes. Their sense of smell decreases quite a bit and they may not notice the smell of their clothes or their bodies as they used to in the past. What your nose picks up as the rose of that flower called "old sweat," they may not even smell at all. Out of smell, out of mind. They may forget how long it's been since they showered or changed their clothes.

They could feel afraid of slipping and falling in the tub or shower. They may fear that they won't be able to get out of the shower or tub once they get in. They may feel embarrassed to ask for help and are mourning the loss of one more thing they can control.

The first thing to do in this situation is to figure out why this is happening. Why did they stop bathing or cleaning their clothes? Why have they lost their sense of smell? Is it from advancing age or from a medication they might be taking?

If it's depression, seek out your network and find the professional help for them. Let their doctor know this is happening.

If they are concerned about asking their child caregiver for help in bathing, it's time to call in reinforcements! Someone else can come in and give them a bath on a scheduled, routine basis. An outside caregiver can be the professional help they need.

If they are afraid of getting in and out of the shower or tub, there are many styles of shower chairs that can be helpful. If the person has dementia and is afraid while bathing, move gently. Don't insist on a full shower or bath. Perhaps just ask if you could wash their face for them, then move on to other parts of their body as they feel more comfortable.

Most of all, stay away from nagging. It is always coun- terproductive. They will only dig their heels in more and be harder to deal with on this subject. A daily bath isn't necessary. Try lowering your standards and definition of cleanliness.

INAPPROPRIATE VERBAL BEHAVIOR

One of the most shocking and disturbing behaviors that our elders could develop is the use of offensive language. As shocking as it is to hear our loved one spewing foul words out of their mouths, it is even more hurtful when it is directed at us.

A Betty White type outburst coming from our elder, who hasn't previously been the kind to use this communication technique, can be upsetting. Cutting comments, name calling, and cursing from our elder isn't like television where we laugh heartily at this behavior or roll our eyes. Most of the time, these comments are directed at the caregiver and meant to hurt.

Keeping in mind that they might be reacting from a place of fear or illness can help. These out-of-character outbursts can be the onset of dementia or Alzheimer's disease. They can also be triggered by a change in pain medications. When your loved one reacts like this, it's important to have a few tools in the toolbox, metaphorically speaking.

The tool of distraction helped me. It's a simple but effective way to divert their attention to something else. Once their mind is redirected, the swearing fit may end. Bringing up happy times from the old days can be an effective way to distract them. They like to reminisce about times gone by. Those times gone by are often clearer to them than what they did yesterday or the day before. Using their long term memory may end the cursing or inappropriate comments... for a while.

Another tool that worked for me was to back away, disappear, and wait for it to blow over. Standing there taking the abuse is not productive for you or your elder. Doing verbal battle with them never works. It just keeps heating the situation up to a frenzy.

THE DIRTY LITTLE SECRET ABOUT HOARDING

The subject of hoarding seems to be a hot topic these days. I can see why. Growing up with it in my family left me ashamed and confused. I didn't want anyone to see the conditions I had been raised in. I was confused about how to deal with it. It was a dirty little secret I didn't feel I had any control over. As my parents aged, the hoarding behavior became much more pronounced.

My parents lived through the Depression. Mom was raised in a very poor situation in Oklahoma. They had dirt floors in their home. Her parents were farm hands. Mom could run mule teams by the time she was seven years old; she could knock a squirrel dead with a rock. Her hunting skills helped feed her family. Even though she was a dead-eye with a rock, there were many nights her family went to bed with nothing to eat. Did she feel the need to hoard because of her childhood?

Dad lived on several farms in southern Iowa when he was growing up. His father was a farm hand until they moved to town, where he became the high school custodian. My grandparents saved everything from wrapping paper and tinfoil to old clothes for quilt making. They were frugal farmers.

Dad's family has kept the furniture my great-great-grandfather made. It traveled down the Ohio River with the family when they moved to Iowa after the Civil War.

When Grandma passed away, they moved all of her things into their home. They couldn't stand to part with anything!

Their home was literally filled to the rafters! Obviously, my family loves their stuff. When does "loving your stuff" cross over into unhealthy hoarding?

Each of my siblings and I had spoken to them about getting rid of some things. That was as well received as a nuke at a peace rally. If you have ever known a hoarder, you know this is a very sensitive subject. My parents were obsessively attached to their stuff!

Their hoarding had become extreme. They had been living in their home since 1963. They kept everything, from junk mail to bags of old walnuts which were probably ten years old, or older.

When Mom's health began to slip, there were numerous ambulance rides. My parents' home had become so cluttered that the ambulance drivers couldn't get a gurney through to her bedroom. They had to take her out in a sling type of cot. When she arrived at the hospital, the trip through the house had been so perilous and close that she had a piece of one of her house plants stuck in her hair. This issue had reached critical mass. We finally had no choice, but to deal with it.

After the first ambulance trip, while Mom was in the hospital, we moved like a united front. We swooped in and cleared away the paper and trash. We filled a dumpster numerous times. I don't know if the way we did it was correct, but it had to be done. My parents were not happy with our actions, but what could they do? This, however, did not stop the hoarding.

As my parents continued to age, they were less able to care for themselves. I became the one who helped them pay their bills, among other things. Then it dawned on me. They couldn't make a decision about the mail they should keep and what they should throw away. Their dementia and Alzheimer's were making it increasingly difficult for them to sort their mail and make decisions accordingly.

While I was dealing with their mail, they would appear nervous, but also relieved. I disposed of the junk mail they didn't need. When I first started doing this, I had to take the trash completely out of the house to keep them from wanting to retrieve it.

I know that when some of my friends have had to deal with their parents' hoarding, it seemed to be spurred on by anxiety. Anxiety about aging, or the anxiety of possibly outliving their resources. They seemed to begin collecting and saving to stave off the feelings of being overwhelmed by what lies ahead. Others seemed to hold on to items because they fear their memories will be lost without that tangible evidence of the past.

In the case of my parents, when they had to relocate to a full nursing care facility, we had to go through everything to prepare their house for sale. We found many treasures, and lots of junk. And, yes, to answer the question I know must be in your mind, great-great-Grandpa's furniture is still in the family.

STRANGE OBSESSIONS AND OCD

Another group of behaviors that seem to be on the opposite side of the spectrum from hoarding but are still compulsive behaviors are Obsessive Compulsive Disorder and other forms of strange obsessions.

What elders obsess about can vary. They could save tissues, worry incessantly about their medications, pick at scabs or flaws in their skin, etc. These behaviors can upset the elderly person and their caregivers. Often this behavior is related to an addictive personality, or they could have a past history of Obsessive Compulsive Disorder, commonly referred to as OCD.

What can be done in this situation is to realize first of all, it's not a character flaw, it's a symptom. It can be related to a number of other disorders, such as anxiety, depression, or dementia. It can be treated by mental health professionals. Make an appointment for the elder to be seen. Therapy and perhaps medication may be the answer. There are therapy groups and inpatient or outpatient programs for this. Check around for these programs. Consult your elder's physician for a referral to a mental health care professional and a program for dealing with obsessive behavior.

Another strategy is to watch for the triggers to this behavior. Certain events or activities may trigger it. After discovering the trigger, try to avoid the event or activity as much as possible. It's important not to participate in their ritual. If you have been participating in the past, it's time to change the pattern immediately. It's also important that family and friends don't participate in the rituals either. Seek out the mental health professional for help.

REFUSING TO LET OUTSIDE CAREGIVERS INTO THEIR HOME

Mom was fine with letting outside caregivers into their home when Dad was still living at home with her. She enjoyed the attention from them and it helped her care for Dad. Once he had to be moved out of the home, she became hostile to those who came in to see her. She kept telling them that she had family to take care of her. I think she was afraid that having a professional caregiver in her home meant her family wouldn't or didn't want to take care of her. I believe she felt more vulnerable to her care needs. She had always fixated on Dad and now it was hitting home that she needed the help.

She needed constant reassurance. It took many chats for it to sink in that they were there to help her. Professional caregivers are familiar with this behavior. If they have been in the industry for very long this won't be their first rodeo! Suggest to your elder to "just give it a try." Have the professional caregiver come in for a few hours a week doing some light housekeeping – the housekeeping that has been difficult for the elder to do. Something where the elder will see a difference and it benefits them. Keep being patient and talking to them over and over again accentuating the positives and reassuring them. Once they become accustomed to the professional caregiver, they may be fine with it.

OVERSPENDING OR EXTREME FRUGALITY

Some caregivers feel like pulling their hair out over their elder's shopaholic behavior. My mother received every health and beauty offer in the world. She had purchased a Jack LaLanne juicer, which she never used. She received boxes and boxes of the mix that went with it. When we cleaned out their home, she had twenty or more boxes of this mix.

She used to sell cosmetics from her home in the 1960s and 70s. She hadn't been signed up with any company for years, but she was receiving boxes and boxes of beauty products every month. They sat unopened around her house. She would throw a fit if I wanted to cancel them.

She bought televisions, health books, elliptical equipment, CDs, DVDs, and anything to do with a healthy lifestyle. She didn't read them, use them, or even open up the box half the time. She was obsessed with the "great deal" she got on them. I tried to explain that it's only a "great deal" if you use them or read them. Her credit card bills became quite high.

Mom2 has an obsession with DVDs. She has to be one of Amazon's best customers. She spends hundreds of dollars every month on DVDs that she watches once, maybe twice, and then they sit around her apartment.

I've come to believe that this behavior is about control, power, and independence. Age is robbing them of all three. They are attempting to retain control of their life in a strange way. "It's my money and I'll spend it the way I want to!" is their mantra. Excessive spending and excessive saving are like drugs that cover up the fear of losing control.

My husband works with family finances in his career. He has had many talks with Mom and Mom2 about their spending habits. Mom2 has the resources, but with the depressed economy, her resources are dwindling fast. My Mom wouldn't listen even when we showed her how much she was spending every month. She thought it was "worthwhile stuff."

When my husband had to invoke the financial power of attorney and I was paying their bills, we took away her credit cards. We canceled the automatically incoming monthly products. It was a battle that she waged with us. But they didn't have the resources to keep doing this. Their credit cards were charged to the limit (which helped cancel the incoming products when the credit card was rejected).

Mom2 hasn't curbed her enthusiasm for Amazon no matter how much my husband speaks to her about the waste in her spending. She turns a deaf ear to him. She believes this is one of her little indulgences since she doesn't shop for clothes any more. Obviously, she has always had a spending issue. She pays off her credit card every month, so she still maintains control.

WANTING ALL OF THE CAREGIVER'S TIME AND ATTENTION

This is a very common and frustrating behavior. A caregiver's time can be stretched very thin, especially if they have a career outside elder care. Our care receiver can feel slighted, feeling like the caregiver won't carve out enough time for them. They can act out in many areas, or put tremendous pressure on the caregiver with guilt.

The elder may not feel well, or be upset about the things they can't do anymore. There are a multitude of reasons for why they feel the way they do. It's important to understand why the elder is responding this way. It's also important to honor our own feelings and time restraints. If we don't, the stress can be crippling.

I've known so many caregivers who struggle with this. This unwelcome behavior strikes very close to home for me. Once I started the intense phase of care giving for my parents, the pressure of Mom's already monstrous appetite for my time was unbearable. She wanted my time 24/7/365. She became all-consuming. Every day was another guilt sandwich, with a side of hostile remarks and a dessert cocktail of anger. Her anger was intense and always present whether I was there or not.

When I was with her, the attitude she gave me was "what have you done for me today?" If I wasn't with her at that moment, she would track me down with hateful phone calls. She would tell everyone she talked with about my failure as a daughter. If you have gone through this or are going through it right now, you know the scenario.

I suffered from "Caregiver Burnout" in a big way. It almost cost me my life.

MOM, YOU'RE MAKING ME CRAZY!

"If you can't change your fate, change your attitude."

~ Amy Tan

My journey in elder care has been a long road with many twists and turns. Many light spots of joy and feelings of fulfillment. As wonderful as the bright spots have been, I was unprepared for the joyless and debilitating feelings of caregiver burnout.

A very scary but true statistic is: 63% of caregivers will die before their care receiver. I never wanted to be a part of that statistic... but I was headed there! Anyone who has been doing the job of care giving for any length of time knows that caregiver burnout can be a brutal reality.

My parents were my first and have been my most high-intensity care giving experience. I love my parents with all my heart. But my relationship with Mom has always weighed heavily on my care giving.

I believe each person's role in the family begins way, way back in the childhood years. At this point, I have to shed a little light on what it was like to grow up in my family.

Dad grew up tall, dark, and handsome in southern Iowa. He was the eldest of two children. They weren't a wealthy family. They were hardworking mid-western farm folks. One of the stories he liked to tell about the Depression years was how his family, after all their needs were met and debts were paid, had a net profit of a dime at the end of the year. He learned early in life about having a strong work ethic. Like many children from that era, he grew up helping his father farm.

My grandpa was a hired hand and they moved often. Dad liked to tell the story of being educated in one-room schoolhouses. In March of every year, many people would have to change domiciles because of the start of the farming season. Many of the people who were hired hands would have to move on to another farm for another job. He often said one of his teachers told him that when she came to school on March 1st, there was only one child who had been with her the day before. Everyone else was new.

Dad's mother, Grandma Bea, had been a teacher. She put off getting married until she was 28 years old because she loved to teach. Back in the first few decades of the 1900s, women weren't allowed to teach children after they were married. She and my grandpa dated for many, many years before she finally decided it was time to start raising her own children. She was a wonderful, loving and progressive woman. She loved to read, wrote stories, and was very active in their community. I spent many summers sitting on the porch swing listening to her read the Laura Ingalls Wilder series to me. She has inspired me and has always been a role model for me.

Dad was quite the "catch" in his area. Not only was he good looking, but he was one of the stars on his school's basketball and baseball teams. After graduation, he helped his father on the farm until he received his greetings from Uncle Sam and was drafted during WWII. This was his first experience away from home. And what an experience!

Uncle Sam insisted he move from the green agricultural beauty of Iowa to the equally beautiful desert landscape of New Mexico, where he was stationed in Carlsbad. He was trained to be a Medic with the Army Air Corps.

Mom was also raised on farms. Her father was a hired farm hand. The difference was, her family was extremely poor. Early on in her life, they were displaced from their home in Oklahoma because of the dust bowl and the Depression of the 1930s. She was raised with dirt floors and bad nutrition.

Mom was the eldest of seven children in her family. When she wasn't caring for younger brothers and sisters, Mom was called on to work with her dad in the fields. She learned to run mule teams by the time she was seven years old. She often told me that her happiest times as a child were in the fields working side by side with her dad. They worked hard and passed the time by singing gospel songs. Music and singing have always had an important place in her heart.

Her mother wasn't a physically healthy person. She suffered from pellagra among many maladies that could have been corrected with proper nutrition. There were quite a few miscarriages between Mom and her next sister. Because of Grandma's poor health, Mom spent many long hours taking care of her siblings. She always said she would rather have been in the fields with Grandpa.

While she was growing up during the Depression, her father was out of work for many periods of time. They lived in squalid conditions, little shacks with dirt floors when luck was on their side. As a small child, she learned to hunt with only her wits and anything handy. She was a sharpshooter with a rock. She could knock a squirrel out of a tree and kill it for supper. She'd find a rabbit and chase it down into its burrow. Once she found its burrow, she would get a long stick and put it down the hole. She'd just barely touch the rabbit's fur with the stick. Patiently, she'd rotate the stick until it had grasped the fur tight enough to drag the rabbit out of its home, bash it on the head and take it home for supper. It was a good day for her family when her hunting was successful, as they would eat that night. Even with her many successes hunting, there were many days when there wasn't anything to eat.

Entertainment for Mom and her cousins growing up was to find a poisonous Copperhead snake basking in the road and stone it to death. She became a strong, fiercely independent and resourceful child with a sharp eye and a deadly aim!

When World War II broke out, Mom followed the jobs. She quit high school. The war was the biggest employer. She migrated to the nearest military base and became a "Rosie the Riveter." She was trained to break down airplane engines.

She met my dad on a blind date. But not on a blind date with each other. Dad had been set up on a blind date with one of Mom's friends. They met at a USO dance. Dad was strongly attracted to the tall, beautiful lady who would become his wife and lifetime partner.

The highlight of the blind date was that Dad met Mom and they became a constant item. After Dad was shipped out to the Pacific, they kept in close contact by mail. As soon as Dad was shipped back to the States, he made his first stop Carlsbad, New Mexico, where he whisked her off for a quick wedding in California before taking his nineteen-year-old bride back to Iowa to meet his family.

Mom's family always lived in the warmer climate of Oklahoma, New Mexico, and California. She felt very displaced and unhappy in Iowa. She missed her family and hated Iowa's cold winters of ice and snow. Dad tried moving us to California. We lived there for six years. We lived in Stockton, which is a very agricultural community, but Dad was allergic to peat. Peat farms were everywhere. It wasn't uncommon for Dad to pull the car over and sneeze ten or more times in a row. In spite of the beauty of California, my memories are haunted by my parents' knock-down drag-out fights.

She was constantly haunted by her own personal demons. The biggest one was her perception of Dad's family as better than hers. These feelings of inferiority were fueled by her lack of a diploma. She didn't get her GED until my third sister was two years old. Instead of seeing that as a success, she used it to build on her insecurities and belief that Dad's mother didn't approve of her. Actually, I don't think that was the case. I believe those feelings were only in Mom's mind. But perception is everything. It led to many bitter feelings on her part.

Mom and Dad began their family on their honeymoon and by the time they had been married four years, they had three little girls. Not only was she living away from her family in a cold climate, but she was once again strapped with raising children.

I was daughter number four in the batting line-up. Dad tried four times to get a son. He desperately wanted to have a son and name him Bill, after his best friend during World War II. Bill was the closest to a brother Dad would ever have. They were both Medics in the Army Air Corps and served their country on the islands in the Pacific.

We have all heard the old saying, "opposites attract." This was the case with Dad and Bill. Dad has always been a quieter guy. He has always had a delightful sense of humor, but wasn't very outgoing. Bill, on the other hand, was a man who lived life hard and fast. He shared Dad's sense of humor, but in Bill's case, he never knew a stranger. He was gregarious and lighthearted. As I grew up, Dad entertained us with many "Bill and war" stories.

At the end of the war, they stayed in close contact and visited each other often. Dad loved to travel and he would pack us all up in the car and head for Arizona where Bill had set down his roots. When I was ten years old, Dad was notified of Bill's death in a small plane crash. Dad was devastated. He slipped into depression and it added to their already strained marriage. In hindsight, I now realize that they were both depressed, for different reasons. Dad spent more and more time at work and Mom was difficult to live with.

As a child, I spent a lot of my time scared and upset. Mom was a volatile personality. She could be loving one moment and abusive the next. I learned to judge her moods as soon as I walked into the room. Her moods could switch in a matter of seconds. She would go from loving and nurturing to mean and spiteful, and come out swinging. Anyone nearby or the object of her rage, would get it.

My parents fought constantly. When I was very young, the fighting always upset me. The yelling was bad enough, but Mom was a thrower. She'd pick up anything close by and pitch it. I don't think we ever had a full set of dishes. We kept cashing in Green Stamps for more china.

As she got older, her mood swings became even more erratic and less predictable. When we had all moved out of the house to start our own lives, Dad became the focus of her rage. His close confidant was his mother, Grandma Bea. She lived about two hours away. He'd take off for the day for a visit. I could see by the time he came home he would be feeling better. The relationship between Mom and my grandmother became even more strained. Grandma saw and heard many things but kept them close to her heart. She didn't want to lose her son and grandchildren.

I eventually learned to deal with all of it in my own way. My sisters never did. Each one of them fled the state as soon as she was of age. They would sometimes come back for holidays, but those visits were troubled truces at best.

Mom's moods would swing in two-week cycles. When I was out of the house and on my own, I could avoid her during the two weeks of anger and abusive behavior.

And then, tragedy struck. Someone broke into my Grandma Bea's house and killed her during a sexual assault. My family was devastated! Dad once again withdrew into the depths of depression. Mom and Dad didn't stop fighting. She still found things to pick at, but Dad stopped sticking up for himself. She respected him less and less.

Fast forward fifteen years. I've found the love of my life, a good and thoughtful man to share my life with. We have our three wonderful kids and life couldn't be better. I was still "dealing" with Mom in my own way. It was working, and Mom and Dad were actively involved in our lives. The kids adored their Grandpa. I kept a watchful eye out for the children's safety.

Then on that hot, humid day in August, Dad had his first heart attack. The chapter in my life's book called "Care Giving" had begun.

As with many life-changing events, it didn't start with a parade and a brass band. It started out with the little things. Dad's heart attack was the pinpoint on the map of my life where my role as their daughter changed. Their dependence began slowly.

About the same time, Dad started needing me to go with him to the doctor. Mom would go, but she spent the time at his doctor's appointment talking about her ills. She was very focused on her own health and imagined ill-nesses. By the end of the appointment she had alienated the doctors.

I enjoyed going with Dad because it gave us time together one on one. I enjoyed our chats. It gave me the perfect opportunity to get to know him better without everything being focused on Mom.

It was on one of these trips that we learned from the doctor that Dad had a condition where the capillaries in his brain were filling up with plaque. When the capillaries become full of plaque, the blood stops flowing to that area and this portion of the brain dies. I'd been noticing Dad slipping in his cognitive abilities. No matter how much I wanted to scream at the world that this couldn't be hap-pening to MY DAD, he had begun his trip down the long road to dementia.

In the fifteen years after Dad's diagnosis, his health and Mom's deteriorated to the point where it became impos-sible to keep them out of the nursing home. Mom has Alzheimer's and Dad has faded into his own little world. In his world, he rarely recognizes me or any member of the family.

WARNING SIGNS OF CAREGIVER BURNOUT

Many of you reading my story won't be able to relate to my relationship with Mom. Some of you will. I know I've felt very alone in my role as care giver, even with my support-ive husband. Those of you in the process of burning out will recognize the signposts of the impending flame-out. Those signposts are:

1. Depression – constant sadness, feelings of hopelessness, crying jags, overwhelming feelings of guilt.
2. Withdrawal – no longer enjoying the things you previously enjoyed, not wanting to interact in social situations, withdrawal from family, friends, and events.
3. Anxiety – about getting things done, or feeling there isn't enough time to get everything done. Anxiety about facing another day and what the future holds.
4. Panic attacks – feeling your heart racing, shallow breathing, feeling like fainting, waking up from sleep with these symptoms and having no idea what woke you. Inability to go back to sleep or trouble falling asleep.
5. Anger – yelling at loved ones more often. Difficulty controlling your temper. Feeling rage flaring up over little things, anger at the care receiver, at family members who aren't helping as much as you feel they should, anger that you are stuck and they aren't.
6. Loss of concentration – constantly thinking about everything you need to do for your care receiver, yourself, and everyone else. Can't keep your mind on your project or job.
7. Changes in eating habits – eating more, which contributes to weight gain, but some people react to burnout by eating less. Both contribute to self-esteem issues, and illnesses occur more often.

8.   Insomnia – exhausted but sleep eludes you. When you lie down to sleep, the mind takes off on its own tangents. Body wants to sleep but the mind keeps noodling on the events of the day or random thoughts. Nightmares, stressful dreams, waking up in the middle of the night and can't go back to sleep.

9.   Exhaustion – waking up in the morning after what should have been a good night's sleep and can't get out of bed from the extreme exhaustion or feeling unable to go on for another day.

10.   Drinking or smoking – doing either one or both, more than previously, or doing them when you've not done them in the past, feeling the need to escape or dull the pain.

11.   Health problems – catching colds or the flu more often, developing serious issues such as heart problems, high blood pressure, cancer, autoimmune disorders, etc.

I was the poster child for all of the above. I was constantly depressed. Dad was fading away and Mom was getting increasingly demanding of my time. Mom's tendency toward being an energy vampire was increasing. She was reacting to the stress of Dad's decline by sucking away any good feelings I had, leaving me exhausted and depressed. I no longer had the option to limit my time with them when she was difficult. As time went on I was around her more and more; the feelings accelerated and intensified.

I was so sad about Dad and his troubles. He wasn't going to get better. I grieved for him. I felt the strain of being everything for them. I felt like things were never going to get better. Our financial situation deteriorated. I was self-employed and my career was taking a hit.

I hate to admit this, but I started to feel like I wanted my parents to die. I wasn't wanting to help them do that, but I wished for them to go to sleep and not wake up. I would have these unholy thoughts and then my guilt meter would hit maximum overload. I was locked into a cycle of serious depression and I thought about dying... a lot. I probably thought about ending it more than I wanted them to die. I felt so incredibly guilty about my "bad" thoughts. I felt like I was going to be trapped in this stage of my life forever.

My care giving had reached the most that anyone can do without having them move into the house with us. Moving in with us was never an option. I'd made a promise to my husband when we first married, that Mom would never be invited to live with us when she was old. I knew my relationship with Mom was such that, if she lived in the same house with me, I would actually cease to exist. I couldn't handle a 24/7/365 handout of abuse and guilt she fed me, and the guilt I fed myself.

I finally reached a stage where I was researching suicide on the Internet. The only thing that kept me here was my family. We had a young nephew who killed himself in his early twenties. I saw what that did to his immediate family and to ours.

About that same time, I lost a dear friend to lung cancer. It happened quickly. She was sick less than six months before she passed. She was only 44 years old! Her children hadn't settled down and gotten married. There weren't any grandchildren to enjoy yet. She was going to miss out on the most important events a family can experience together. I had an epiphany! I realized if I did such a thing, I would hurt my children and my husband irreparably. I also realized I didn't really want to die. I wanted to see my kids get married and have my grand-children. I wanted to be a part of their everyday lives. I couldn't do that if I wasn't here anymore. It was a wake-up call for me!

HOW TO PREVENT OR RECOVER FROM BURNOUT

As I related earlier, I got very sick with a heart condition. I had absorbed all the stress I could. I needed to fight back to wellness and that meant getting some help. Here are some things that worked for me.

FIND SOMEONE TO TRUST:

In my case it was Dad's Veterans Administration social worker. She knew my situation with Mom. She had seen her in action. She had the training it took to help me. I talked with my husband and kids; they listened, they understood, but I think I looked at them as being preju-diced to my side of the story. It helped to get the outside view and some professional help. I highly recommend talking with a professional – a counselor or your pastor. An Aging Advocate service, a doctor, or a professional care giving service can steer you to a professional who can help.

TAKE A BREAK:

Use the respite and health care resources available. Find a service that can help with bathing, grocery shopping, and housekeeping. Get away for a weekend; let someone else stay with your care receiver for a while. When things were the worst and I couldn't handle it, I called my sister and asked if she could arrange her schedule to take Mom to a doctor's appointment. She had to make a three-hour drive each way to do this for me, but she did it without complaints. Ask someone for help.

FIND A SPECIAL PLACE FOR "JUST YOU":

It's important to find time for respite. Time for the caregiver. It's also important to have a special spot. It can be outside in a park, but having a special space in your home can be important too.

Care giving of any kind can quickly take over our lives. When my children were little, toys and baby care items quickly became strung all over the house. Adult care giving can be similar. Especially if a 24/7/365 situation is going on in our loved one's care. It's easy to have the walkers, canes, breathing devices, oxygen tanks, etc., sitting around in every free space and table top all through the house. Even people who are exceptionally organized can find their existence 100% impacted by elder care.

I believe it's very important to have a space in the home that is dedicated to the caregiver. It doesn't have to be a big space. It could be a small area with a rocking chair and anything soothing. For me, I have an area with my grandmother's rocking chair which is now mine, and a nice sunny window surrounded by some house plants. I can go into the room, shut the door and sit and enjoy some music, gaze out the window or look at some of my house plants that I enjoy. If I choose to close my eyes and relax, I can. I'm free to practice my meditation. I know a mere ten minutes in my special place can do wonders to relax me.

This is something that needs to be discussed with the care receiver. Not for approval, but to let them realize that when you are in your special place it should be respected, and the time you spend there should also receive respect. It's best to go to our special place when we know our elder is in good hands with someone else available to give them care, such as when the professional caregiver comes in to bathe them.

This makes our little retreat a worry-free area. The most important part of making a space for ourselves is it should be a guilt free zone! When relaxing in our special retreat place, we should never, ever spend one second of time feeling guilty about anything.

"JUST SAY NO!" TO STRESSFUL AND DRAINING SITUATIONS:

Even if they are happy events and situations. Someone else can be responsible for the holiday meals or planning the family events. It doesn't have to mean forever. Even when it's a previously enjoyable task, it can be overwhelming with care giving responsibilities. Both sides of our family have always enjoyed being at our house for family events.

We have the right set-up for entertaining. It's been what my husband and I have always done for everyone. I found out that passing the torch can be a blessing in disguise as others will learn what you do to put on these events. I've learned to kick back and let others stretch their wings and have these events.

FORGIVE YOURSELF:

This step is very important. In my life, I held on to all the things I felt I had done wrong and beat myself up over them again and again. I've never been an unforgiving person, but I was to myself. For me, depression was anger turned inward. Learning how to forgive oneself can be a difficult but powerful lesson. I believe being locked into lack of forgiveness for ourselves leads to unhappiness, disease, depression, stress, anxiety, self-deprivation, addictions, and a host of other unhealthy situations.

IDENTIFY WHAT I CAN CHANGE AND DON'T WORRY ABOUT THE REST:

Worrying is a robber of life. I found that if I'm worried about something, it steals my joy and feelings of well-being. I've learned, when I find myself worrying, to ask myself, "Is this something I can change?" If it is, I work on changing it. If I can't change it, I let it go. I ran across a method of releasing called The Sedona Method. It was easy to learn and made perfect sense to me. This method helped me learn how to release my worries.

SET REALISTIC GOALS AND EXPECTATIONS:

Many large tasks can be broken down to smaller, more manageable tasks. A large task can seem overwhelming if we don't break it down. "Inch by inch, it's a cinch."

I also found that it's important to be realistic about our care receiver's prognosis. Hope is always important, but unrealistic expectations can derail us. For instance, it didn't help me to expect Dad to come back from dementia. It's upsetting in the long run to have unrealistic expectations. It's better to enjoy the bittersweet good days. Knowing those will be followed by bad days. It's okay to enjoy the good days without having to shake our fist at the bad ones.

PRIORITIZE:

Make lists and establish routines. It's easier to stay on task and more can be accomplished with a list. Number the list by importance. If something stays on your list for more than three days, perhaps it's not important... strike it from the list. Keeping unaccomplished things on the list has its own power to drain our productivity.

ESTABLISH AND STICK TO A ROUTINE:

Establishing a routine is important. There are so many things to do each day for our elder. Medications to give, treatments to administer, the list goes on... It's easier to remember everything we need to do if we know one thing follows another. A nice perk for an organized routine is that our care receiver finds a routine comforting.

The only drawback to a routine is if it becomes an excuse to be inflexible. A routine is a progression of events, not a timetable strictly adhered to.

JOIN A SUPPORT GROUP:

Ask your loved one's doctor, social worker, or any other professional caregiver for a lead to find a good support group. They have been asked for this before and may have other people's feedback on what the groups are like. They understand your issues and have experience in this area.

I'm not much for joining outside groups. My time is limited, and I found online support helpful for me. There are some wonderful forums out in cyberspace. Other people have had the same problem and have found a way around it or through it. Internet support groups are great because I can tap into them in the middle of a sleepless night, or whenever I have the time.

EAT RIGHT AND EXERCISE:

I know you are saying, "Yeah, right!" I know this is an easy one to fudge on. It's handy to grab a sugar snack instead of a piece of fruit. I know, because I did this. I didn't think I had time for a walk or any other activity. I would grab donuts or another unhealthy snack because it was handy.

I didn't realize what I was doing to myself until I was overweight and my blood pressure was through the roof. I lived in a perpetual state of high blood pressure. Which, by the way, is a silent killer. That pesky headache can be explained away by sinus trouble and the current weather change. Sometimes there are no telltale signs of high blood pressure until a stroke hits.

I put off my physical exam because I didn't have time. I developed an unexplainable rash. The discomfort sent me to the doctor and I discovered my blood pressure was in the stroke range. That scared me! I headed to Weight Watchers Online. I dropped 30 pounds. I still have more to go, but it's a good start.

DO YOUR RESEARCH:

Do your research – find out what resources are available and what your care receiver qualifies for. Knowing in advance keeps the stress levels down. There are many aging advocate agencies available in your location that can help you discover what's available for your situation. They can help you fill out paperwork and send in applications. Choose one that doesn't cost out of pocket. Many agencies are compensated by the different services they hook you up with. Their knowledge is epic and extremely valuable.

TAKE A BREAK:

When care giving gets stressful and the breaking point feels close, consider taking a leave from your job. There is something called the FAMILY AND MEDICAL LEAVE ACT. Research it and see if it's a fit for you.

LEARN TO MEDITATE:

This saved my life. When I started, I had no idea how to meditate. My sister told me it would help and I was willing to try anything to feel better. I found this website that helped me learn the art of meditation. Here's a link to a meditation course for busy people: http://www.mind-bodytrainingcompany.com/go.php?af=1038314.

I started out with "mindfulness" and progressed to meditation. It amazed me how much stress was lifted off me by practicing meditation daily.

DEVELOP A PROTECTIVE SHELL:

I made a decision; I wasn't going to let anything my mother said to me get to me. Sounds easy, doesn't it? It's not. I developed a ritual in the morning to protect myself. I would sit quietly for a few moments and visualize zipping myself up into a positive shell, similar to an egg. Mine was filled with pink light and surrounded me with love. Anything that wasn't loving bounced off the shell and couldn't get inside to me.

When she said unkind things, I would mentally picture the comment hitting the shield and bouncing off. Whether it's a visualization or just an attitude, the peace of mind and freedom come from making the decision not to allow anything to hurt. I released myself from the bondage of allowing anyone to cause me harm by their words or actions.

If we continue to allow someone else to upset us, we are a victim. A victim doesn't have any control of a situation, or of their life, for that matter. Victims aren't strong. They aren't survivors. They don't have a hand in their own destiny. They are buffeted by the winds of other people's making. I choose to live a life of my own design. It doesn't mean that I won't help others and am wrapped up in myself. It means I choose to help them; I'm not forced by situations out of my control.

Once I did this, I can't tell you how much better I felt about myself and my life.

CULTIVATE A SENSE OF HUMOR:

Learn to laugh. I have a dear friend who always says, "The funniest things happen to the funniest people." That comment sounds a bit rhetorical and silly, but it's true.

When I realized that I was the one who could find the humor in things, it lightened my mood and how I saw my role as a caregiver. I'm not suggesting laughing in your care receiver's face. I'm saying look for the humorous moments. Mom didn't have much of a sense of humor, but often I could help direct her to the humor of the situation. We could laugh about the little things.

Dad has always been an inspiration for me with his keen sense of humor. He loved to laugh. He enjoyed laughing at himself most of all. He was like this until the dementia became so pronounced that he doesn't know us most of the time. As he fades away, so does his humor. I will always treasure the moments we spent enjoying the lighter side of life.

ATTITUDE IS EVERYTHING:

When I was going through all these things, I knew I

needed to change. I realized I was locked into a cycle of negative thinking. I had difficulty setting boundaries in my relationship with my mother. The blame wasn't hers. I couldn't go on blaming her. If things were going to change, I had to change. As I said, I chose to help them. My life was where it was because of the choices I had made. I was the one putting the negative spin on my life and my care giving. One of the things I realized I could control is my attitude and how I look at the different things in my life.

One of the problems with negative thinking is its ability to self-perpetuate. A negative thought leads to another negative thought, which leads to yet another negative thought. This continues until we are consumed by them, and suffering from the evidence of their passage through our minds and into reality.

Here's the game plan that broke my cycle of negative thoughts.

PRACTICE MINDFULNESS:

When I started to feel really depressed and blue, I would stop what I was doing. I would look at what I had been thinking. As a newcomer to mindfulness, it took a full-blown depressed attitude for me to realize I was causing it. There was always a direct correlation between my depression and the thoughts I had been thinking. If this sounds unbelievable, try it. As I got better at mindfulness, I began to be able to notice the negative thoughts in their infancy.

A word of warning here. When you are practicing mindfulness, don't expect all your thoughts to be hearts and flowers. There can be some pretty ugly stuff brewing in that gray matter. Don't feel guilty, just work through it. Mastering mindfulness doesn't mean never having another negative thought. Negative thoughts have their place in our lives. They give us contrast. They happen. They let us know something is going on that we may need to address. They shouldn't be feared or banished completely from our thinking. They are signposts letting us know there is an issue to be addressed.

I knew I wanted to be happy. By watching my signposts I could change my thinking and lighten up on myself.

TALK BACK TO THE NEGATIVE THOUGHT:

After recognizing the thought as one which didn't make me happy, I would say "stop!" Then, I'd begin to find ways to be less negative about it. A way to put a different spin on it. Sometimes, it was just a little step up the ladder to a more positive thought. A slightly less negative perception of the same thought. I got better and better at this until I could turn the thought around and see a positive one to put in its place. I realized I may not be able to change the situations I was in, but I could change how I saw them. Negative thoughts attract like thoughts, as do positive thoughts. I realized I couldn't hold two opposing thoughts at the same time. I couldn't think positive while having a negative thought in my mind, and the reverse is true. My situations changed for the better by utilizing a positive outlook.

Modifying Thoughts:

There are six negative thought patterns caregivers can get into.

All or nothing thinking – This is a very black and white kind of thinking. If our performance isn't what we think it should be, we see ourselves as failures. It might be just one thing, but we expand and multiply it. One single unpleasant event turns itself, in our minds, into a continuing pattern of defeat. Words which point to all-or-none thinking are words such as "always," "every," or "never" – generalizing isolated mistakes or failures into the ultimate defeatist attitude.

This example of negative all-or-none thinking happened to me.

I was late picking up Mom for her doctor's appointment. The roads were slick and I got stopped behind an accident and unable to move for fifteen minutes. When I got to Mom's, she wasn't quite ready. By the time we reached the doctor's office, my fifteen minutes ahead of schedule turned out to be ten minutes late. The lady at the front desk rudely informed me that I would have to reschedule because we were ten minutes late. Arghh! My inner voice was screaming, "I'm such a loser! I'm always late!"

I discovered a more positive response would have been, "I'm not always late. There are plenty of times I'm on time or early. Sometimes circumstances beyond my control make me late and that is not a reflection of who I am as a person."

Discounting the positive – In the past I was very hard on myself about my accomplishments. I would dwell on what I perceived as my negative failures. I would over-look the positives as not important and focus on what I thought I'd done wrong. I would tell myself, "I'm not a good caregiver." I would let the guilt eat away at me. I finally realized and started telling myself, "Care giving isn't always easy. It's a tough job that takes strength and compassion. I'm not always perfect; no one is, but I do my best."

Eeyore's law – Looking for the things that are going to go wrong. Always looking for the worst to happen, like Eeyore, Pooh's friend. For instance, "Why bother to try to get someone to come in and give Dad a bath. He won't like them anyway. He hates everyone who tries to do anything for him."

A better way to look at it is, "I can't predict whom Dad's going to like. He may not like the new professional car-egiver, but it's worth a try. I'm sure they've had cranky elderly patients before. I'm sure they will know how to work with him. I bet they'll have some good advice on how to get Dad used to someone else bathing him."

"Should-ing" all over myself – We have our list of rules and expectations we and others should follow. When others break these rules we get angry. When we break them we feel guilty about it. We tell ourselves "we should do this," "we shouldn't do that." We think telling ourselves these "shoulds and shouldn'ts" will motivate us, but in actuality it de-motivates us. When it's in conflict with what we really want to do, it frustrates us and trips our

guilt meter. Do it too many times and we start disliking ourselves for it.

A negative I've heard so many people say, and I've said it myself, is about exercising and weight. "I should exercise right now. If I don't work out I'm just going to keep getting fatter." It turns exercise from a pleasurable way to spend our time into an obligation or work. We're punishing ourselves with our image of getting even fatter, flooding our mind with negative thoughts.

A better way would be to say, "I'm in the process of losing weight and improving my health. Even though I accept my current weight, I'm looking forward to feeling even healthier. I'm going to do an activity that I enjoy, like walking. I love getting in shape!"

Sticking a self-imposed label on our chest – When we identify ourselves with a characteristic or action. Calling ourselves names, such as "terrible person," "lazy," "getting old," "getting fat," etc. We speak to and about ourselves in a way we would never talk to another person. We are demeaning and disrespectful to ourselves. Saying: "I'm so lazy because I don't feel like cooking," when instead we could say, "I don't feel like cooking today. I like to cook sometimes, but today isn't that day. I feel like relaxing and taking a break. I work hard and deserve a frozen pizza night! Or better yet, let's get delivery!"

Making it personal – Taking responsibility for every failure or negative circumstance when it is beyond our control. It's a good thing to take responsibility when we haven't done the right thing or acted in a positive manner.

It becomes a problem when we take responsibility for things we can't control. Saying things like, "Mom has to go to a nursing home because I'm a failure as a caregiver." Instead, we could say, "I have taken good care of Mom for the past three years. Her health has reached the point where she needs constant medical supervision. It's the condition of her health and not my care giving that requires her to be in a nursing home."

Acknowledging negative self-talk as destructive behavior is one thing. Halting it and choosing a more positive way to talk to ourselves is another. The first step is to recognize it when it is happening in your head. What is that little voice telling you? Re-framing our thoughts to a more positive spin can work wonders in how we feel about our care giving and ourselves.

PARTICIPATE IN LIFE AGAIN:

I began to participate in life again. I developed some new interests in life and cultivated some of the ones I had previously enjoyed. I stopped pushing my own guilt meter if I wanted to enjoy something that was unrelated to care giving. I utilized some of the services from the Veterans Administration to take care of Dad, such as bathing and adult day care. I made a point to stop feeling bad if I asked someone else in the family to do something for Mom and Dad. For me, that was the hardest thing. I've had the sole caretaking responsibilities, in my nest of siblings, for Mom and Dad. It was tough to acknowledge that I needed help and then to ask for it.

CULTIVATE THE RELATIONSHIPS FROM THE PAST:

Only the ones which made me happy. I didn't seek out the ones who made me less than happy. I have a tendency to avoid people and issues that make me uncomfortable. This was an advantage for me at this point in my life. I began to get out and meet some new people.

EDUCATE AND LEARN:

I read self-help books and anything I could about mindfulness, meditation, how to pursue positive thoughts, law of attraction, dealing with depression, elder care, etc.

STARTED A JOURNAL:

I learned I could release my feelings through the written word. It gave me the ability to reread my thoughts and look for patterns, such as people and situations I allowed to depress me. I could see the actions, mine and others', that caused the depression to worsen.

FUN PROJECTS:

I found that starting a fun project such as making a family calendar helped me feel better and productive. I enjoy writing. I started a blog using my expertise in the business world. I feel a sense of accomplishment when I see what I've written. I really enjoy it when people respond in a positive manner to my writing.

Some people enjoy crafts, or getting involved in an online course to help them enjoy more positive thoughts.

Being able to incorporate a healthier lifestyle is a plus. I love to walk. I started out walking short distances with one of my dogs. I worked up to walking three miles a day. I enjoy being outside, feeling the breeze in my hair. I feel like I'm gliding along! It gives me a special time to think, away from everything else. I enjoy thinking about the things and people I love. I enjoy counting my blessings on my walks. I've made my walks another "no guilt allowed, worry-free zone."

If I start a walk with negative thoughts running around and around like a hamster on a wheel, I stop and remind myself what "zone" I'm in. Reminding myself, and the act of walking, snap me out of it.

There are so many fun projects out there to choose from. Here are some other things to chase the blues away and keep those negative thoughts at bay.

STAY BUSY:

 Staying busy can be a big help in keeping the negative bugaboos away from your mental doorstep. But this can cut both ways. If I stayed too busy it added to my sense of anxiety and perpetuated depression. I found that it's best to stay cognizant of that and not get stretched too thin.

LEARN TO BE PATIENT WITH MYSELF:

I had to learn to be patient with myself. I've always been harder on myself than on anyone else. I realized it's easy to be my own critic. I needed to lighten up on me! I began to practice forgiveness for myself and others. Feeling better takes time. I had to give myself the time and practice a lot of self-love.

If you're like me, sometimes doing something nice for yourself takes a back seat to the needs of others. This is altruistic and noble, but can add to negative thoughts and depression. Respite for the caregiver is a must!

When home health care is involved, it's possible to leave the house for the time it takes the home health care worker to bathe, toilet, and dress our care receiver. This gives you an hour or so of time to do something for yourself. Use this time to enjoy yourself.

Adult day care can also be an option for getting some time to ourselves. The Veterans Administration was the one to suggest this and paid for two days a week for Dad to attend an adult day care. This gave Mom and me a break.

At first, he was unhappy with this situation. He didn't want to go anywhere or be with people he didn't know. After a few visits, he was enjoying himself. He got to talk with other people in the same age group, the World War II boys! The day care always had ways to keep them interested. They would play games to sharpen their minds. They went on field trips. They went outside and walked with Dad, which was his favorite thing to do. They had coffee and treat time where the older people could sit, talk, and reminisce.

Here are a few more respite activities a caregiver could enjoy:

1.   Have a cup of tea, cocoa, or a flavored coffee.
2.   Read something you enjoy! I know many people read for work and become tired of reading, or they don't read well. In that case, listen to a book. It's important to enjoy what you are reading.
3.   Spend time with your pet, loving and petting your furry friend. People who have pets are said to live longer. Pets are always loving, and enjoy the time spent with them as much as we enjoy that time. They are great listeners. They don't judge us. They are the purest form of unconditional love!
4.   Garden; inside or out. I enjoy my indoor garden... my house plants. Spending time digging in the dirt, re-potting them, pulling off the dead leaves and blossoms always relaxes me. It's heated and air conditioned in my home. I don't have to sweat, swat bugs, or get sunburned. I'd tried to do some outside gardening, but things don't grow very well in the shade! Those darn bugs think I'm their personal landing strip! Each of us is different. Choose what is best for you.
5.   Feed or watch birds, or fish. Take your dog to the dog park. Their antics can be smile producing! Spend time in nature.
6.   Enjoy a bubble bath or shower. Turn on your favorite soothing music, light some scented candles and relax! Make sure your care receiver is being taken care of so you can spend carefree time in the tub without interruptions.

7. Escape with a television program or movie. Comedies are my favorite. I love to laugh. Lose yourself for a while!
8. Don't forget to make that private "you" spot. A rocking chair in a private location, a deck with a view and a comfy chair, or a big boulder in the backyard to sit and think. Some place that can be completely yours.
9. Call a friend who makes you feel good. Don't dump all your problems on them. Talk about something you have in common that isn't about your care giving responsibilities.
10. Surf the net for fun or to plan an outing.
11. Take a nap. This is especially important for those caregivers who are getting up all throughout the night caring for their loved one. An uninterrupted nap can be a wonderful and blessed thing.
12. Trade off care giving with other family members. This only works if you are willing to leave the guilt behind.

DEFEATING THE "ENJOLI SYNDROME"

There seems to be a syndrome that affects a lot of caregivers. It can be very detrimental to their health. I've suffered from it. I call it the Enjoli syndrome. Enjoli is a perfume made by Charles of the Ritz. Back in the 1980s it was very popular. The commercial was about the 8-hour perfume for the 24-hour woman. The ad said this scented woman could "bring home the bacon, fry it up in a pan, and never let you forget you're a man, because I'm a woman!" Even though most of us don't remember the perfume or the commercial, we are still trying to be everything to everyone. This syndrome has been called "Superwoman." If you're a male caregiver, the syndrome is still there. Just picture the man in the blue tights with the big S on his chest. We want to be there doing it all. The problem for those of us who have been affected by this psychological pressure is the intense burnout it can cause.

NEWS FLASH!! We can't do it all. No matter how loving, caring, organized, and just plain awesome we are, it's not possible to do it all... and survive.

Why is it so hard to let go? Even when we recognize the need to take a break and get away, why can't we? I believe caregivers get caught up in the "I need to be in charge of everything that has to do with my loved one's care." This is a dangerous way to think. Sometimes, we think that care giving has a certain set, short length of time, and it stretches out to months and years. Thinking we have to be in charge of everything is a recipe for burnout.

I've heard and felt that "I can't stop worrying that something will go wrong if I'm not there or I don't do it." Our brains run away with the "what if" scenarios. "What happens if Dad has another stroke while I'm gone?" or "What happens if they wake up and the respite care giver doesn't hear them?" These thoughts make enjoying our respite impossible.

The all-time champion killer of enjoyment when we need to get away is, "I shouldn't be enjoying myself while my loved one needs care." This is guilt doing our thinking for us. These thoughts make relaxation impossible. The next step is care giver burnout.

Some of us have extreme difficulty asking for help. In my own situation, I sometimes wonder if I thought people would perceive me as weak and ineffectual. One reason I was reluctant to ask for help was that I didn't know how or where to get this much-needed help. I did my research and talked with my gurus of care giving and found some tips that saved my bacon... and I didn't have to fry it up in a pan!

Here are some additional tips for breaking the "Enjoli or Superman syndrome":

MAKE THE DECISION THAT YOUR LIFE MATTERS!! – Caregivers are notorious for letting their health or their life go. Where's it written in any caregiver handbook that we need to sacrifice our lives for theirs? We use ourselves up with the care for another and then feel guilty because we haven't done enough, or guilt because we would like to enjoy our lives. How can we want this when they need us so much? The only way to let go, relax and live is to decide your life is as important as the life of the person you are caring for.

WHEN YOU DECIDE TO TAKE A BREAK... BE GONE!! – Leave and enjoy yourself. Only a dire emergency should reel you back in. It's important to note, it's harder for a caregiver to relinquish the "I've got to fix it all!" attitude than it is to really know that our lives are just as important as the life of our care receiver. We really can't fix it all, no matter how much we wish to. We can help them be happier, healthier, and more comfortable. When it really sinks into our hearts that we can't fix it all, then we can leave and truly relax for however long we have for our break away. When you decide to be gone, it's very important to do something you really enjoy. When we are enjoying ourselves it's more difficult to get stuck in the guilt and what ifs.

LEARN AS MUCH AS YOU CAN ABOUT YOUR CARE RECEIVER'S CHALLENGES – Do the Internet search, talk to their physician, join a support group that deals with this particular challenge or set of challenges, for instance Alzheimer's groups, Parkinson's groups, cancer support groups, etc. Learn the proper way to transfer your care receiver if they are fragile and wheelchair-bound. Learn hands-on skills for preventing and treating pressure sores; how to give injections, handle catheters and feeding tubes, set up wheelchairs, and everything about how to deal with their oxygen needs. There are many caregiver resources available through the Internet and books with this information. Learn things like tax strategies for saving money. There are deductions that can be taken for their care. If your loved one is going to be using hospice services soon, find out everything possible about hospice care and research the different facilities in your location. The more prepared we are, the less likely something will come along and derail us.

RESEARCH AND FIND MOBILE SERVICES THAT CAN HELP YOU OUT – Whether it is getting your pet groomed or veterinarian services, they can be handled remotely. Many towns have groomers who will pull up in your driveway, come in and get your dog, take it out to the van and give it the full beauty treatment. There are some veterinarians who also provide this type of service. Many hair stylists will come to the home and take care of you and your loved one. Some physicians for the elderly have started making house calls for shut-ins. In-home nurses can come to the house and draw blood and do vitals. Grocery stores will shop for you for a small fee. Our local grocery store would shop and deliver without a fee if the order was put in at the same time as the prescription order. When shopping, most stores welcome the opportunity to have an employee help in the aisles and put heavy things into the car on your shopping trips.

BE PREPARED – When someone shops for you, if you aren't familiar with the store ask the store for a blueprint of where things are located; or if you know from personal experience where things are, your grocery list can be written with this in mind. This keeps your helper shopper from having to backtrack all over the store to fill your list.

Keep a list in a central location such as the outside of the refrigerator so items can be added to keep up on what's needed. On the list, put in the brand name if you have a preference, whether it should be fat free or sugar free, etc.

Check into volunteers at church or elderly centers for shopping helpers. Look under "Errands" in senior resource directories.

Check with an aging advocate service or Veterans Administration for housekeeping helpers.

Check with Meals-On-Wheels to see if your housebound elder qualifies for their meal assistance.

We can work on self-improvement and having more positive thoughts. We can read up on and join some online forums to understand our care receiver's behavior. This can help us live with our sometimes (or all the time) cranky old person who seems to be hell-bent on making our lives miserable.

Why are they so mean, hateful, and unreasonable? How can I learn to deal with it?

I related to you how Mom's progression to her "Alzheimer's mean self" took place. Often, a person can be difficult before the start of dementia becomes evident, like Mom. Old age can intensify traits that are already in their personality makeup. The caregiver is the person they take their negative behavior out on.

But what about the person who was not this way previously? Why do they lapse into abusive behavior? I believe it's the fear and uncertainty that exacerbate such behavior. They are frightened that they can't take care of themselves. They are frustrated that they have to depend on someone else for what they used to do themselves. They have lost resources, the ability to function on their own, and most important, their independence. They are responding in a self-protective survival mode.

If we can find out what fear has taken control of them and address their concerns, often the unwelcome behavior lessens or stops. If it doesn't, it could be time to nip it in the bud and let them know how they are behaving. Talk to them about their attitude in a respectful way.

When someone is frightened or angry, they don't always realize how they are foisting abusive behavior on the ones they love. They don't recognize how this is affecting their caregiver. A person with dementia may not have the presence of mind to stop their behavior. A professional could help in this situation. A therapist could help our elder work through these feelings in a much more productive way.

If your elder won't go to see the professional... you go. The therapist can help you work through your own feelings the behavior is causing in you. They can help you with the oxygen mask on the airline of care giving that's dangling in front of you. Are you going to grab it and put it on your face?

Remember, it's a loving thing to help a dear one in the winter of their life, when they are heading into the home stretch. We must never forget, our life is important too. We have a life to live. We must remember to live it! It's all for nothing if we go before them in death. It doesn't help them and it definitely won't serve us to die early.

THE LEGAL NUTS AND BOLTS OF GROWING OLD

"We must take change by the hand or rest assuredly, change will take us by the throat."

~ Winston Churchill

I believe we all would like to have control of our own lives, well into our golden years. How do we preserve those freedoms? We all know, especially when dealing with elder care, that a person can lose the ability to make their own decisions. This can happen as quickly as one illness, stroke, or coma.

The best way to preserve our freedom is to make our own decisions early, before disaster strikes and we are unable to do so. It isn't enough to make the decisions and then count on your family to carry those decisions out. These decisions need to be in legal form.

When my parents were still active and mentally with it, they had their directives made legal. They've never been financially well off. There wasn't a large estate to deal with. They wanted to preserve what they felt was important in their golden years. Even without a large financial estate, there are many things to consider and prepare for.

I'm not an attorney. I can only tell you what my parents did to ensure their wishes were honored. It is up to you or your parents to seek out legal representation to discuss options.

My parents didn't have the money to hire an attorney. They were living on social security and a very small monthly investment. They contacted the legal department of the university in our city. They had their legal documents drawn up by law students and checked over by a professor, who is also a lawyer.

POWER OF ATTORNEY

They drew up a Power of Attorney (POA) to take effect if they were unable to make decisions for themselves. Mom named Dad as her POA and he named Mom as his. If the other wasn't able to serve in that capacity because of death or mental incapacity, my husband would become the POA.

The reason they chose him for this important job was that I didn't want to serve in that capacity. I wanted to retain peace in the family, if something should happen to them. My husband is a trustworthy person and we all trust him.

It is important to have two different POA documents, independent of each other, for each person. There is the financial power of attorney for making all the financial decisions should the individual become incapacitated. There is also a power of attorney for health care directives naming a person, and a back-up person, who will make the health care decisions for each individual. It's very important to have a will and a living will for each parent.

When the documents have been drawn up, check for accuracy. It is easier to change them at the time they are written, than to try to change them at a later date. For instance, there's been some confusion because my mother's name was spelled wrong on the document for the Power of Attorney for health care. It hasn't caused a huge fuss, but it would have been better if it were correct.

As it turned out, Dad had to go to a nursing home first. His health deteriorated until he was cycling in and out of the hospital about once a month. He became so weak he would fall at home a couple of times a day. We tried a six-week stint at the VA physical rehabilitation, but it wasn't successful. Finally, the VA said he would have to go to the Iowa Veterans Home. They weren't willing to place a full-time care giver in the home.

By this time, Mom was suffering from dementia. She had lost her capacity to retain short term memories. When Dad was out of the home in a full nursing home facility, she was disoriented. I was very worried about her. She wasn't eating. She was receiving Meals-On-Wheels, but her weight loss was dramatic.

She couldn't remember where Dad was. She had delusions and hallucinations of all of my sisters and me coming into her home and physically taking Dad away. She thought we had kidnapped him. She would work herself up into an angry frenzy! When she would have a few lucid spells and remember that he had gone to the Veterans Home, she would threaten to go get him and bring him home to live.

Whenever she saw me, she'd fly into a fit of rage and threaten to hurt me. At that time, my husband and I decided to send in more services and keep our contact to a minimum. It wasn't good for anyone for me to be with her.

Her ability to care for herself diminished quickly. I made daily calls to her home care nurse who came in to take her vitals and check the pill box. Her nurse was very concerned about the rapid deterioration. I turned to Mom's doctor and told her what was going on and she sent a referral to the agency that was taking care of the in-home nursing services. They sent a social worker/psychologist out to make an assessment. My poor mother was so disoriented that she didn't know the date or year. If we hadn't had the POA drawn up in advance, it would have become a court issue.

She didn't want to leave her home, but the dangers were apparent to everyone. I was concerned about her adjustment to living in the Veterans Home. She has always been a shut-in without friends. I thought the adjustment to people around might be too much for her. I was pleased to see that she is very happy. I haven't seen her this content for as long as I can remember.

It still amazes me how quickly the anger left her once she moved to the Home. She has become serene and peaceful.

I believe it has a lot to do with taking the right medications, and taking them on the right schedule.

It was a painful ordeal for everyone. If we hadn't had the POA drawn up in advance, it would have been an even more painful legal process.

I'm pleased to say, my relationship with Mom has changed again. She is content with her living arrangement. She's happy to see me again. We have nice visits. It is a long drive for us to visit. I still have other elders to care for here in town. I'm also blessed with the most amazing little grandson! I get to babysit him a couple of times a week while his Mama goes to school to finish her degree.

When I get the opportunity to go see Mom, I want her to remember that I was there, if possible. Her short term memory isn't good and she doesn't remember when I was there. I try to make our visit memorable. When I visit I take her flowers, or a very small plant, or a small gift of some kind. She has limited space, but she has always loved her plants. When I take her flowers, it helps her remember that I was there.

WILLS OR TRUSTS

Once again, I am not an attorney. You should always seek counsel from an attorney. What I can tell you is that having a will is extremely important. It is the way to have your intentions honored.

Many of our parents are in possession of family treasures. They also may have an estate with money involved. A will is important. If they should die without one, their estate will land in probate and can be tied up for anywhere from six months to years. With a will, their wishes can be upheld without the cost or help of a probate court. When there is money or property involved, professionals with this experience should be contacted.

Mom2's second husband died without a will. He had two grown sons from a previous marriage. He had been wise enough to put Mom2's name on his possessions such as the house. She had put in half the cost of several remodels to their lake home. In the state they lived in, the wife was entitled to $600,000 worth of assets without a will. There were still some details that had to be settled in court.

The attorney costs are much higher going through the probate courts than if their services were used to draw up the legal documents beforehand. Death is not a good time for a grieving family to go through legal issues. Adding the possibilities of bad feeling from a court battle is hard for any family to withstand.

When drawing up a will, it is best to put an addendum with it, laying out in black and white, who should receive what. This helps keep the family squabbles from flaring up over the family treasures.

When a couple has quite a few property assets, putting them in a trust might be a good solution. Only a lawyer familiar with a couple's assets and needs, can answer these types of issues. Seek professional help.

LIVING WILLS AND HEALTH DIRECTIVES

Living wills and health directives are important for honoring our wishes when we are incapacitated and can no longer say how we would like things done. Living wills on file with your doctors and hospital can give the proper direction you want in your own care.

It is a good idea to talk with your care receiver and see what they feel they want. Do they want heroic measures taken to keep them living and breathing, no matter what? Or, if they aren't going to get better, do they only want to be made as comfortable as possible and allow nature to take its course?

In the state where I live, only the spouse can override a living will at a hospital. Mom did this when Dad went into cardiac arrest. The hospital had put on his chart a DNR which is a DO NOT RESUSCITATE order. She couldn't stand to let him go. It might have been a bad decision on her part, if he had not come out of the coma. He lived and had at least eight more years of a decent quality of life. This is why it is so important to communicate your wishes to your loved ones.

PREPARATION – WHAT TO HAVE ON FILE

It is always good to be prepared. If possible, help your parents set up files. My parents aren't organized. We bought them a safe for Christmas one year. Some of the things we needed were in the safe, but there was a lot we had to search for when the time came.

Some people are very private. They don't want anyone knowing their business, including family. If they are open to help, and to letting you know where things are and what they have decided, here are some things to make sure you have.

1. Know where their wills are located
2. Where their Social Security cards are (the actual cards)
3. Know what their health insurance covers and their cards and numbers
4. All the bills should be in both names if possible, in case of death
5. Have signed POAs, wills, health directives completed and know where they are kept
6. Know their Social Security numbers (or where to find out this information) and birth dates including year of their birth
7. Know the location of their birth; city, state, and hospital
8. Know where their birth certificates are kept
9. If your parent was a veteran, know where the discharge papers are located
10. Know where they keep (in a safe and secure place) codes and PINs for all accounts
11. Copy of their Union cards if applicable
12. Know the benefits from their Union or Associations (such as burial plots, Union pensions, etc.)
13. Be familiar with their insurance policies such as life, auto, home (where are they kept, amounts, and companies)

14.   Be familiar with their long term care policy. Know who their long term care provider is, length of time it covers, daily amounts covered, and what it covers

15.   Know where the titles are for vehicles, boats, toys, deeds to house, deeds to vacation home, abstract to their homes, etc.

16.   Have they reduced benefits on any policies?

17.   Have them put you down as the person to talk to for credit card bills, life policies, bills, etc. If this isn't done, you will have to file POAs with the companies, before you will get any help

18.   Know where they keep their bills

19.   Know whom the family treasures go to

20.   Know where lock boxes are kept. Lock boxes may be locked down upon the death of the owner of the lock box.

21.   Have a key or combination to their safe of important papers

These are important things to know in case of stroke or inability to communicate.

FOLLOWING THE MONEY TRAIL

Some people's financial situations are very simple. They rely on Social Security for 100% of their monthly income. Other people have Social Security and some form of investments. It is important to have all their investment information in a secure location. If anything happens where a POA is called into service, it is extremely important for the POA to be able to locate all the financial information.

Sometimes older people will stash money in odd places. They may have a favorite cookie jar or teapot. They might even stash it in books, family bibles, certain drawers, or coat pockets.

A couple of my friends found when they checked with their state's treasurer, that their parents had uncollected funds from some financial institutions. One friend found money that had been reported to the state as abandoned from a bank. No activity had been reported on the account for quite some time. Another friend found some money that a Mutual Fund company reported to the state as abandoned. Our state calls it the "Treasure Hunt" and lists all the names in the paper once a year. It's worth checking out.

I have found from personal experience and talking with others, that most people don't have all their information in one accessible spot. They have a little scattered here, and some over there, while most of it is in this one drawer, maybe. It can become a true treasure hunt of a different kind for the individual designated as having Power of Attorney! Here are some financial matters to become familiar with.

PENSIONS, IRAs, 401k, OTHER INVESTMENTS

There is nothing more frustrating for the designated POA than not knowing what financial investments and financial instruments our care receiver may be using. It is important to have the information secured and in a place the POA has access to.

Lock boxes may be secure, but unless the Power Of Attorney's name is also on the lock box, they may be locked out. Many people choose to use fireproof safes. I have even heard of people who keep their important documents in their freezer. They think they are fireproof and safe from theft. Wherever these important documents are kept, their location should be told to the potential POA.

The important information to be able to locate is listed above, plus: their Social Security information (this includes their Social Security benefit page which is mailed to them every year), any account numbers for their investments, names and addresses of the financial companies they are doing business with, name and phone number of their broker, actual policies or shares, pension information, 401k providers information, all their property holdings, and anything else which is financial in nature.

BILLS AND EXPENDITURES

It is important to know where your senior keeps their bills and checkbook. If they are hospitalized or have to go into a care facility and the POA is invoked, the designated POA needs to know where this information is located. They may need to pay the bills or check on energy bills for the house. Keep in mind, if the POA is not invoked and no other person is on the checking account, no one can sign the checks and pay the bills.

Other expenditures which happen on a regular basis need to be recorded and the pertinent phone numbers available. They may have a regular Swan Foods delivery once a month or Meals-On-Wheels. Any goods or services that are coming into the home on a preset regular basis, such as water softener salt delivery, etc., need to be recorded.

Many of our elderly don't file taxes because their Social Security income is too small to report. But for the ones who do file and pay taxes, be sure to know the individual who does their taxes, find out where their past returns are filed, and the location of the information they have collected for their current tax year.

Our care receiver, if they pay taxes now, will have a tax return due in the year in which they die. When considering inheritances, this is an important fact to remember. If they have taxes to pay, the money may have to come from the people who inherit from their estate.

PREPAID BURIAL AND PLOTS

When Dad and Mom went to live at the Veterans Home, even though they lived on a small fixed income per month, they still had some money that needed to be spent down. Their assets had to be below $2,000 each. If their assets were above this threshold, the cost of their care would be bumped up to the next level. This is set by government regulations. Those regulations can change at any time.

One asset was a cash value policy my father had purchased at the end of World War II. None of us knew he had this policy. When the Veterans Home was doing their financial background checks, they found it. They suggested that we buy prepaid burial plans for my parents.

This was a real eye opener for us. We were able to arrange a very modest burial plan for each of them and the cost was very close to $10,000 apiece! This is not including the actual burial plots. They already had their burial plots, which they had purchased years ago from the Union Dad belonged to. The deed to their plots was in their safe. It is a must to know where these deeds are located!

Two years later, we were arranging the funeral of one of our elders we care for, and the cost of burial without the plot or headstone had gone up over $2,000.00! This was another eye opener for us. It's becoming increasingly more expensive to bury someone. For this reason, prepaid burial insurance can be a wise expenditure. When we purchased the plans for my parents, it included everything: flowers, caskets, vaults, cost of printing, obituaries, preparing the body for burial, transportation of the body, etc.

It is important to have a handle on what your loved one wants for a funeral. How big do they want it? What kind of funeral do they want? Some older people have already planned their funerals. The songs to be sung. The bible verse they want shared. Mom2 has her obituary already written. Some elders find it reassuring to have these wishes known. Some feel it's ghoulish and don't want to know or be involved in the preparation of their funerals.

Mom2's second husband wanted to be cremated. He had a spot already paid for at Fort Snelling. His burial site was in the part of the cemetery reserved for cremation. His deceased wife was already cremated and buried there.

Mom2 outlived him. If he hadn't told her in advance, she might have planned a different resting place for him. This would have jeopardized the burial site for his previous wife. Fort Snelling's rules for interment insist the veteran is to be buried there with their spouse. His deceased spouse was not a veteran. If he was not buried with her, her ashes would have to be removed.

It may sound morbid, but it is important to know what your loved one has planned, or is wanting.

If your family member is a Union member, it is best to check with the Union to see if there are plans put in place for their burial. In Dad's case, his Union had gone belly-up and all of the benefits went with it.

Another place to check for burial funds, if your parent is a Veteran, is the Veteran's Administration. Every soldier gets a set amount for burial. Our state has a beautiful Veterans Cemetery.

Yet another source can be life insurance. Even if they have stopped paying on it, it could still be in effect, with some reduced benefits.

There are many different financial situations. Many people are not organized and the path to unravel their situation can be mind boggling! It is best to know in advance what your loved one's situation is. Unraveling it before death, or before mental deterioration takes over, would be the easier route to take.

ELDER-PROOFING THEIR HOME

*"If you judge people, you have no time to
love them."*

~ Mother Teresa

As I mentioned earlier, my parents were blessed to be able to stay in their home for quite some time. I found that the older they became the more unstable they were in their mobility. I never had to think twice about child-proofing my home so my toddlers were safe, but it never occurred to me to make sure my folks' house was elder-proofed!

After the hospital visits started happening, and more services were brought into the home, that's when I got the education on elder proofing. Older people, because of their diminished eyesight and their unsteady mobility, fall much more than younger people. They can trip over a rug that may have been there for ten years or more! Many of them take blood thinning medications and a fall could turn into a life-threatening event. It is very important to make sure their environment is as safe as possible.

AGING IN PLACE

Baby boomers are aging. They're also the largest group of people ever to go through the aging process. Moving that many people through the aging process at the same time is like pulling a pig through a garden hose. There will be lots of adjustments to make on every aspect of elder care. Since there are so many people destined to hit the senior age group at one time, more companies are starting to pay attention to the phenomenon known as "aging in place."

"Aging in place" is terminology for tailoring our homes to meet our changing needs brought on by the aging process. If we are able to change our home environments to make it easier to accommodate the extra needs of a person growing older, it only makes sense that we can stay in our homes longer.

Needs for aging in place would be things such as: larger doors that are better suited for wheelchairs and walkers; showers stalls that can be walked into instead of stepping over the side of a bath tub; lever door handles instead of doorknobs, making it easier for people with less dexterity to access a room; lever type handles on sinks to accommodate the arthritic hands, etc.

There are many things we can do as weekend projects to change the home into a friendlier environment for our aging elders. Changing doorknobs on kitchen cupboards to something easier to use. Putting extra lighting in dimly lit areas. Changing doorknobs to handles. Putting up grab bars in the bathroom. Removing all throw rugs and loose flooring.

This trend has spread to home builders, who are now building homes to accommodate those who are aging. They have been able to incorporate the needs of the elderly into the design of the home. They have gone light years beyond building a ranch style home without stairs. Many builders are saying they can build an elder-friendly home with as little as 3% to 5% added to the cost of the home.

Consumer Reports has a ten-question interview with Michael Thomas, an aging in place expert who can answer more of your questions.

FALLS

Falls can happen to even the most cautious people of any age group. The elderly have more falls than any other age group. As our parents age, their eyesight isn't as good as it used to be. Their gait may be more unsteady. Their muscle tone isn't as good as it once was. Medical issues and medications can also add to their fall risk.

Many falls happen because elderly people may not be able to bring themselves back to a stable upright position from a misstep. Their leg muscles no longer have the strength or flexibility to compensate. If you have ever watched an older, less stable person walk, they tend to take small baby steps. They may watch their feet with their head down. This can lead to more missteps and falls.

It's very similar to driving a car. If we don't look far enough up the road, and are only looking at the end of the hood of our car, we will have more accidents. We aren't looking ahead to see obstacles in our path or the big picture. We will be all over the road and can drift into any lane without being aware of it. Elderly people, when walking, will react the same way, but without the muscle tone to be able to right themselves, they fall.

There are many ways to help our elderly person with this. If they have become home bound, or have had a hospital stay, with a doctor's referral Medicare will pay for most of a Physical Therapist's time to come in and develop an exercise program for them. The Physical Therapist will focus on strengthening their leg and arm muscles. Even a short time with a Physical Therapist can make all the difference in their mobility.

Nursing homes also have Physical Therapists on staff to help residents strengthen those much-needed muscles. Elders can get physical therapy in a nursing home on an outpatient basis. It may be better for them to stay in a nursing home for a short time, to regain strength.

Dad had quite a few short term stays in nursing homes to strengthen him after a hospital visit. He spent six weeks in the Iowa Veterans Rehabilitation Unit to help him become stronger. The therapists worked with him on ways to compensate for dizziness, such as not moving his head a certain way.

I found a great website with helpful exercises that are tailored for the elderly: Exercises For Persons 60 Years and Older. It has easy-to-understand language and pictures, with different levels of strength and expertise. You may want to check it out: http://orthoinfo.aaos.org/topic. cfm?topic=A00237#Warm%20Up

Another great way for our seniors to stay fit and flexible

is using yoga. Often our seniors are unable to get down on the floor, or back up once they are down there. A wonderful website I found is Chair Yoga for Seniors: Video Series. It is a step-by-step video series for seniors where they can comfortably sit in a chair and practice yoga. Yoga is great for strength and flexibility. There are some advertisements on each video, but it is worth waiting through the ads. http://www.ehow.com/videos-on_3786_chair-yoga-seniors.html.

There are many obstacles which can lead to falling in the home. We should be on the lookout for rugs in the walking paths. Many people want to save the wear and tear on their carpets by putting down runner rugs. These runner rugs can become lethal to our oldsters. It is better to remove them before they lead to a fall. Likewise, ALL loose rugs and mats in walking areas, such as welcome mats, bathroom mats, and bedroom throw rugs, should be removed and not used.

The same holds true for cords that run across their walking pathways in their home. My parents used a portable heater on their three-season porch, which allowed them to use the porch in the winter months. They would plug it in with the extension cord running across the walkway. I'd move it and discuss with them why it wasn't a good idea to have the cord running across their path. The next time I came over, it was back again across the walkway. They had a reason to do it this way, but really it was their way of having some control of their environment. Not until Dad fell on it did they realize the wisdom of moving the cord out of the walkway.

My parents always kept a yardstick behind their cupboard. One day it fell out and Dad tripped over it and took a header! Any obstacle that sticks out or over where they walk is a fall waiting to happen.

Mom loves her house plants. She could get them so close to where they walk that they too became a fall hazard. Chairs that are not pushed up to the table are a risk.

Furniture should be arranged carefully allowing for a clear walking path. Coffee tables can be big offenders. They can get pushed up too close to the couch and can be tripped over.

Watch out for furniture with sharp corners or edges. Remove the offending furniture altogether, or pad it when possible.

Remove things that tip over easily. Our stubborn elders, who refuse to use a walking aid such as a walker or cane, will reach out to grab on to something as they are walking. They grab on to furniture or walls. If something they grab tips over easily it can send them sprawling – things like rocking chairs, hat racks, potted plants, and plant stands. Rocking chairs can trip them if they get too close to the back where the rocker sticks out.

Many falls take place in bathrooms. It is imperative for anyone, not just our senior citizens, to have non-skid surfaces in the bottom of the tub. A non-skid mat can be used and then pulled up and hung to dry. Non-skid decals could be used in the bottom of the tub or shower, but they can become unsightly from mildew that collects around them.

No senior citizen's bathroom is complete without grab bars on the wall beside the tub and toilet. With so much hard porcelain around, a bathroom fall could prove to be disastrous! If they are not installed properly, those wonderful handholds could turn into a detriment when a fall occurs.

With increased age-induced changes, and increased weakness in their arms and legs, it may become difficult for elders to keep their shower regimen going. Mom didn't seem to be as clean as usual, and she started remarking that she was feeling insecure about her safety in the shower. Even with grab bars and non-slip surfaces, if elders are weak, they could still get stuck in the tub or on the toilet, or take a fall.

A safer way to use soap in the shower or tub is to use the plastic bottles of liquid soap with a pump, or soap on a rope. A safer shower is one with a shower curtain. If they have a glass door in their shower, it is so easy when they fall to go right through the glass door.

Be wary of any spilled water, whether it is droplets from the shower or a spilled glass of liquid. It can turn any hard surface, such as laminate floors, waxed floors, slick finished tile, etc., into a skating rink of disaster! Even a few drops of water can be enough to cause a fall. Take care to wipe up all fluids on the floor. Our bathroom floor has a textured tile. It is much easier to walk on than any slick finished tile, but it is still slippery when wet. For a good rule of thumb, if your pet can slip on it so can you!

Pets can be our loved ones' friends and companions. Too often, these four-legged loving companions weave in and out of their person's legs. They can walk so closely in front of elders that they become a tripping hazard. The lack of flexibility can make it more difficult to step over their furry friends. It is important to teach pets to stay out of the walking zone of anyone. Dogs can be trained to give our elderly people room to walk.

Cats are a different story. They can be trained, but it's not as easy. Mom2's cat was always winding around her legs on the way to the kitchen. That scares me to death! He finally learned to ride on the seat of her walker. Her trip to the kitchen is a lot safer and more fun too! We all love our pets very much, but our aging parents and we, the caregivers, will have to be even more vigilant not to fall over them.

Another area to watch is stairways. It's easy to start stacking things on the stairway in hopes that the next person going up or down will take it to its appropriate location. After a while, when the items keep building up, we have a falling issue in the making. In my parents' home the stairway was always treacherous. They used it as a pantry. The older they got, the less they ventured upstairs. Whenever it was necessary to go upstairs it was horrible experience!

It is a must, not only to provide handrails on all stairways, but to use them – even if there are only one or two steps. It is important to have a sturdy handhold. Having a too-small handhold or a wimpy one is more dangerous than not having one at all. What a dangerous and shocking experience to have the handhold come off in our hands or break when putting pressure on it!

Patios and decks should have a railing of at least 36 – 48 inches tall. This is especially important if the deck or patio is not level with the surrounding ground. It may sound silly to have railing around a patio slab, but getting too close to the edge of the cement and falling off can lead to broken ankles and other injuries.

We should always check the lighting in our elder's home. The hallways and stairs may not be light enough for them to see if their eyesight is dimming. It might be time to install more lighting to brighten up those areas. It is also important for certain areas to be lit all the time. A trip to the bathroom at night without illumination is a fall risk.

Most people don't realize that wall-to-wall carpeting can be a hazard for our older people, especially if it is too thick. It is easy to catch a shoe on it and go for a tumble. Mom always complained about how she felt so insecure walking on her wall-to-wall carpet. She said she felt like she was walking on the top of a big marshmallow. She was very unsteady and had to hold on to all the furniture as she walked. She is now in a care facility with linoleum floors, and she is much steadier when she is walking. She is also using her walker more because there is more room for her to move around with her walker.

Wall-to-wall carpet can also be a hazard to our elders who have allergies, COPD, and other respiratory ailments. It can be responsible for many airborne particles such as dust and pet dander.

It is important to be aware of the shoes our elders wear. Mom2 was having difficulties with a pair of shoes. This popular brand of shoes is excellent, but the shoes she was wearing tipped up at the toe. They were not made for someone with balance issues. When she walked, she would pitch forward because of the way the shoes were made.

It is important for our less steady people to avoid wearing loose-fitting shoes. Some people find wearing a tie shoe can be uncomfortable because of swelling, or they aren't able to reach down and tie their shoes. If that is the case, Velcro-strapped shoes would work as long as they are fastened tight enough not to slip off their feet. Mom2 and I were at the dermatologist and she told me, as we walked in, that her shoes felt like they were going to slip off her feet. She was feeling unsteady. When we sat down, I noticed that the Velcro wasn't strapped on tight enough. I redid them, and it was a whole new feeling for her!

Shoes such as loafers, strapless shoes, clogs, flip flops, and crocs should be avoided. It is too easy to slip out of them or have them turn on the person's foot and cause a fall. Some people need to wear a slipper due to foot issues. In that case, it is best to get slippers with non-skid bottoms.

If your elderly one is still living independently, a good suggestion is to move some of the things they use frequently to a lower shelf. This removes the need to stand on a chair to reach something. Save the high shelves for items they don't use often or ever. If they absolutely need something on a higher shelf, it is best to ask someone considerably younger to reach it. Place a sticky note on the shelf they can still reach, telling them not to go any higher without asking for help. At least have a safety stepladder with the non-slip surface on the steps and the safety handholds.

Another falling situation can be in their yard. If they leave hoses and cords unwrapped and lying around, they could trip over them. The garage has a virtual plethora of dangers! My Dad put things on the rafters that would sometimes get dislodged and fall down.

Until Dad was 85 years old, he would sneak out of my mother's sight and climb the ladder to clean out their eaves spouts. Mom would get so frustrated with this, she finally called and had gutter toppers put on to keep the leaves out of the gutters altogether!

Safety is not just about their homes. My husband and I were out to eat with Mom2 one evening and a blind man's cane had fallen into the walkway. I'm sure he didn't realize it was a danger, but I saw at least two people trip over it while we were eating. Pay attention and watch your senior walk, and be prepared and in place to give them a steady arm to hold on to.

Keep a watchful eye out for those hidden "trippers." They can be dangerous things. They may be hard to spot because they have been there for long periods of time. We can have a tendency to forget they are there.

Another area of concern is the use of their walking devices such as canes and walkers. There is a technique to using them correctly. If they are used incorrectly, an elder can trip on them. Dad got to an age where he needed to use a walker all the time. He didn't want to use it and would walk off without it. When he was using it, he used it incorrectly and fell with it. It took help from a physical therapist to show him how to use it correctly.

There is a right way and a wrong way to offer support to our elder who has ambulatory issues, when they walk. It is best to talk with a physical therapist about the correct way to assist them with walking.

Which brings us to the wheelchair. If your loved one is using a wheelchair, always make sure the foot rests are up and the chair is locked before he or she gets in. Believe me, I had forgotten this step the first time I helped Mom into a wheelchair. I won't forget again.

Speaking of sitting down. Did you know, it's possible for your loved one to be injured plopping down into a chair or onto the toilet? I didn't, until I did my research. Compression fractures of the spine can happen when they drop down to sit on a chair or toilet. A well placed hand in the middle of their back can help ease them down into the chair. Electric lift chairs/recliners are wonderful in helping prevent this problem in the chair. They rise up to meet your elder's bottom so there isn't a jarring fall into the chair. There are also hand rails for toilet seats available. Mom used one, and the handholds helped her get on and off the seat.

To better assist them in walking, or helping them get up once they have fallen, you might need a gait belt.

Wikipedia describes a gait belt as, "a device used to trans-fer people from one position to another or from one thing to another. For example you would use a gait belt to move a patient from a standing position to a wheelchair. The gait belt is customarily made out of cotton webbing and a durable metal buckle on one end. The gait belt is worn around a patient's waist. The purpose for this is to put less strain on the back of the care giver and to provide support for the patient." They are reasonably priced and I have included this link to Walmart's gait belts: http://www.walmart.com/ip/Posey-Gait-Belt-54/10716043

If your elder is living with you, and they are frequently up in the middle of the night to use the bathroom, it may work out best to have an alert pad under them. It will sound an alarm when they get up. I have heard of people using bells that dangle from a doorknob. Similar to the ones which can be purchased at a pet store, they are placed around the doorknob and hang down. A dog can ring the bell with its nose to let you know it wishes to go outside. Putting that type of bell on our elder's doorknob will let us know they are up and moving around. Falls frequently happen at night when they are a little confused and fuzzy from sleeping. They may need help getting up and out of bed in those instances.

Watch out for anything that radiates heat. Things such as stoves, crock pots, fireplaces, fireplace doors, barbeques pits, grills, or any other appliances should be secured, so our elderly person can't fall into them. Pans on the stove should always have their handles turned toward the middle of the stove. When a fall happens, the elderly person may have enough momentum going that they can fall into those hot objects. One fall into a hot object can compound the danger of the fall.

If your aged person is dealing with dementia, it is time to install locks on windows and doors. Just because they have never tried to crawl out of a window before, doesn't mean they never will. They can change so much after dementia settles in. They become very single-minded. They set their mind on something and they can fixate on it. They can set their mind on odd things like sitting on the windowsill to catch a breeze, or thinking they can fly. Assume nothing. Dementia is a game changer.

One of my worries with my elder loved ones has always been about when they are home alone and fall. Mom2 is having trouble with her balance and she falls. She fell a day ago and was unable to get up off the floor for over an hour. Of course, as fate would have it, she was a long way away from her portable phone. She wasn't able to call for help. She ended up sitting on the floor, bleeding, waiting for someone to come over. I was calling her phone over and over. She was relieved when my husband showed up and helped her get up. She suffered two black eyes and a scraped and broken nose.

Even after this series of falls, she wants to stay in her home. We have done the research regarding the "I've fallen and I can't get up" type of alert systems. There are several companies in this business. The prices range from $20.00 - $46.00 with different bells and whistles. Some have the button secured on their arm like a watch and some come with the button on a cord to go around the neck.

The company she decided to go with is Phillips Lifeline, which is in the higher price range. The reason we chose this service is because it provides a monitoring system that can actually tell when the person has fallen. In the event they are unable to push the button, the company is still alerted and can communicate with the fallen person. If there is no response from the person who has fallen, the company will put in a call to 911 for an ambulance.

The day after this service was installed, she fell. The Phillips Lifeline service was on it! They called my husband and it was early morning and he didn't have his phone with him. They called me next, and I was also away from my phone. By the time I called them back, they had already called 911 and dispatched an ambulance. It was good to see the service in action. I was impressed! My husband and I have learned to take our phones everywhere with us.

The last area of concern I wish to bring up is something many don't think about when our elders fall. Elderly people often take many different medications. Many of those drugs have side effects that include dizziness. When a medication or a combination of medications with this particular side effect is taken by our senior, a whole lot of dizziness can be going on!

I know this is the case with Mom2. With each visit to her different doctors, I brought their attention to her dizziness issue. I wanted to know which medications might be eliminated or changed to decrease some of the dizziness. We were able to weed out five different drugs. Her blood pressure was falling too low and her blood sugar was dropping below the safe range. Dropping those medications helped her quite a bit.

If you don't get any satisfaction there, I suggest visiting the pharmacist. Pharmacists should be very familiar with each medication your elder is taking. Maybe, just maybe, some of those drugs could be changed, or put on a different schedule, or even eliminated to help them be steadier on their feet. It's worth a try!

Everyone's home can be a recipe for disaster. It may sound odd to you to be so vigilant about it. We can try to prevent falls, but they will still happen. If you have done your best, and your loved one has fallen and was injured on your watch, don't beat up on yourself. As the old saying goes, "sh*t happens." We can't prevent every fall.

WHAT TO DO IF THEY FALL?

Okay, since we know we can't prevent every fall, what should we do when they do fall?

Before Mom2 got her pacemaker/defibrillator, sometimes when we would be walking into a restaurant or going into a store, she would start to feel strange. She said it felt like a "sinking feeling." She never passed out, but she would fall, and there was nothing she could do to stop it.

As was our custom, we liked to shop. We decided to go to a large department store. I had dropped her at the front door. As I drove off to find a parking place, I looked in my rear view mirror and she was doing her little dance. Her little dance reminds me of a cartoon character who has been hit over the head. First they go one way, and then stumble back the other direction.

I quickly pulled into a parking place, which, thankfully, was close. I jumped out of the car and raced across the parking lot to try and catch her before she fell. It felt like slow motion. I caught up with her between the double sliding doors, just as she hit an immovable door-sized window. She bounced off as I came up and caught her around the waist. I asked her if she was okay, and she said, "Nope, I'm going down!" All I could do was try to ease her descent. I ended up wrenching my back and she still fell hard onto the rough carpet. She ripped her hand and bruised her knees and shoulders.

The store employees helped so much. They bandaged her wounds. Mom2 refused when they wanted to call 911. In hindsight, we should have taken that ambulance ride and gone to the ER. They would have discovered her heart problem sooner. Several months and a few near falls later, we found out her heart was slowing down and stopping. It would then start up again, slowly. The danger in this is not only from the falls, it is also from the blood clots that can form during these little episodes. Blood, if not moved constantly around in our bodies, can pool and form clots that can go to our hearts, brains, or lungs. This can cause strokes or/and instant death.

I called her cardiologist and we went in for an appointment. He put a heart monitor on her and her problem was discovered. She was a prime candidate for a pacemaker/ defibrillator. The pacemaker part of her device is constantly in use, pacing her heart. Her defibrillator has never kicked in, but should she need it, it is there.

When our loved ones have falls, it is a sign that something is not right. Falls can be caused by many different problems. They can be a sign of a brain tumor, a drug side-effect, a circulation issue, etc. It may seem like we should all know this, but people will often just "suck it up" and keep on trucking. A trip to the ER might save their life.

911 should be called if we are unable to get a person to their feet. Caregivers can have back issues if they try to lift something, or someone, too heavy for them. Paramedics can help when they are called. Always remain with your fallen person. In case of head injury or spine injury, don't try to put a pillow under their head. If you have a blanket, put that over them to reduce shock symptoms.

If your person loses consciousness, always call 911 and make a trip to the Emergency Room.

Also, keep in mind, old people can have brittle bones that break easily. They can have little hairline fractures of the skull, neck, and spine. These can only be detected by an X-ray machine and a doctor. These little fractures can cause problems later if they aren't diagnosed and treated.

If your loved one is heavy, don't make the mistake I did. Don't try to lift them or stop their fall. Paramedics are used to lifting and helping get older people off the ground.

Most of all, remain calm, even if you don't feel that way. Your elderly loved one may be feeling silly, or frightened, confused, hurt, or many other things. They will pick up your attitude. If you are freaked out and not calm, it just adds to the problem. It never helps to get angry or fuss at them. Even if they did something that you feel you have a right to chew on them about, don't do it then. Wait until later when it can be discussed without high emotions.

Sometimes when they have fallen, they can be confused and disoriented. It can really ring their bell! If they act confused, speak clearly to them and make eye contact. It helps clear their confusion. Stay with them, but let them remain where they are for at least five minutes to allow their mind to clear.

If your loved one reports dizziness, or seems to slur their words, or is nauseated, call 911. Many serious issues such as stroke have these symptoms.

If they have fallen and hit their head, check their pupils to see if they are the same size. If they are not the same size or are unusually large or small, call 911 and have them transported to the Emergency Room.

After they've had an opportunity to rest and become less confused, you can check them very carefully and tenderly for broken bones. Ask if they are experiencing any pain. Press gently on their limbs and ask if this causes them discomfort where you are touching them. If no pain is reported, and you can see there are no obvious broken bones, you can slide a pillow under their head. If possible, slip two pillows under their legs. Allow them to rest for five to fifteen minutes.

After they have rested and are feeling okay and not nauseated or dizzy, you can attempt to help them up, only if they are ambulatory. Get a chair ready for them to sit on when you get them up. Position their feet correctly and then help them get into a sitting position. If their feet aren't positioned pointing straight ahead, when they sit up it can break their leg bones. Squat behind them, and bear hug them around the waist. Slow and easy, rise up with them. Keep checking to make sure their feet are positioned correctly. Have them sit down in the chair. If at any point they report feeling dizzy, in pain, or nauseated, stop trying to get them up and call 911 for assistance.

If your loved one has poor ambulation or is non-ambulatory, you will need assistance, unless you have a Hoyer Lift available. If you have assistance, get a blanket folded in half lengthwise. If the lift is available, use the sling instead of the blanket or sheet. Gently roll the person on their side and place the rolled part of the sheet or blanket as close to them as possible. Slowly and gently roll them onto their back.

Go around to the other side and feel under the person for the roll of blanket or sheet and unroll it toward you. This should put them in the middle of the blanket or sheet. Any reports of dizziness or pain yet? Okay, then you can attempt to put them in a position to get them up.

If they are a short distance from their bed you can drag them on the blanket closer to their bed before attempting to lift them. If they are a longer distance from their bed you and someone else will have to carry them in the blanket like a sling to get them over to the bed. You and your helper should squat and grab a double handful of blanket or sheet. Have one person at the feet and one person at the head. It is important to count and move together. Very slowly, stand and lift them. When you are standing, carefully move them to the bed.

Once you have moved them onto their bed, let them rest before attempting to remove the blanket or sheet from underneath them. Place a pillow under their head and two under their lower legs to slightly elevate the legs. If you are able to take their blood pressure, wait a few minutes and take it. It might be a little high from the excitement. If their blood pressure is lower than normal, call 911.

Recheck their pupils for unequal dilation, overlarge pupils, or overly small pupils. It is now time to assess the damages. Elderly people most often have very delicate skin that tears easily. They are sometimes on medication that makes it more difficult for their blood to clot. Check their skin for tears, breaks, scrapes, etc. If you find any, they can be cleaned up with a saline solution and a gauze pad.

When it's time to bandage, remember their delicate skin. Use an antibiotic ointment and apply it to the gauze pad. When dressing the wound it is better to use paper tape, because it doesn't tear skin when it is time to remove it. There is also a mesh type bandage that wraps around the limb and sticks to itself, but not to the wound. Wrap it around after you have applied the ointment and gauze pad.

If the wound is still bleeding, apply pressure by holding a 4 x 4 bandage to it or apply a pressure bandage. Only clean the wound after it has stopped bleeding.

Expect bruising. It will help to put an ice pack on it; this will help with the pain and minimize the bleeding under the skin.

After all of this, your loved one will be tired. They should rest a minimum of two hours if they seem okay. If they fall asleep, awaken them every 20 minutes and check their pupils for the next few hours. If they are hard to arouse, call 911 and have them taken to the Emergency Room.

It is best to call their doctor and report the fall. Falling can be a symptom of something else. The doctor may want your elder to be transported to the Emergency Room, or come into the doctor's office for a visit, or stay at home.

It is important to watch your loved one for at least 48 hours after a fall. If there is a lot of pain, more than just from bruising and local soreness, if the pupils change, blood pressure changes, there is more confusion than usual, slurred words, etc., call the doctor for advice or take them to the Emergency Room to be checked out.

It's important for you to feel comfortable with this. If you don't feel as though you can deal with it, call 911 and allow the paramedics to help. It is their job and they are trained to know what to do.

Remember, falls can be a sign of something else. Any fall should be taken seriously! When the elderly person falls, little bits of plaque can be shaken loose in the arteries and veins, which can cause a cerebral incident (TIA or stroke) or even a heart attack.

Falls can cause fractures of the vertebrae; these are very common. They should be followed up by an orthopedist ASAP! These fractures are painful and can make the patient more off-balance and prone to fall again.

When my parents and Mom2 fall, it is very stressful to me. I know falls are common, but I always feel like I could have done something more to prevent those nasty accidents. I know elderly people fall. It is not my fault. I just have to stay vigilant and pay attention, always!

SEASONAL CHANGES

Changing seasons bring other issues with them. We live in a state that receives lots of snow in the wintertime. In the last years of my parents living in their home, winter was a scary time of year.

My husband and I took care of the snow and ice removal. If we weren't quite quick enough, my father would sneak out and scoop the walk. After his heart attack, my Mom dropped the hammer on that activity. No more snow removal anywhere! I kept the ice melt by the door with a cup in it for sprinkling it around to defrost the pools of ice.

Seasonal changes can mean swapping out wardrobes to bring out the right seasonal wear. A great way to keep your elders off the chairs or ladders while getting at those pesky clothes, is to buy some plastic tubs that will slip easily under their beds. This makes it so much easier!

Winter brings Christmas. Does that mean climbing on ladders in the snow to put up the lights? Where is the neighborhood handyman's number??

Spring brings spring cleaning. Do they have to climb over stairs to get to windows to wash? A call in to their neighborhood handyman will be better than a broken hip on the stairs. Did we find the number yet?

FIRES

When my parents were still living in their home, they had a fire on their three season porch. Mom had left a candle burning. Dad walked out to the porch and found it engulfed in flames. The flames were near the candle, but it wasn't the candle that caused the fire.

My parents had lived in their home for over 40 years. They were using the same electrical cords and extension cords for years. The fire had actually started from a nest of cords that was lying under the table where the candle was sitting. They had their TV and VCR plugged into extension cords. The cords got hot and sparked. The sparks caught the carpet on fire and then spread.

Dad discovered the fire when he walked out onto the three season front porch. Mom was upstairs at the time doing some straightening. Instead of calling 911 to report the fire, Dad, who has dementia, crawled up the junk-covered stairs to get my mother. Thankfully, he had closed the door to the porch and the fire stayed contained in that area. Mom called the fire department. I don't know what would have happened if they hadn't caught the fire as soon as they did.

Our parents had many fire hazards lying around. Candles were left unattended. Fireplaces with creosote buildup in the chimneys can cause chimney and roof fires. Space heaters can last a long time in a household; they can become a fire hazard with bad wiring or when plugged into old extension cords. In the United States, more wintertime fires are started from faulty space heaters than from anything else!

One thing to keep in mind: if your parents are starting to take that short walk down the road toward dementia, their judgment won't be as good as it used to be. Their ability to reason is compromised. Things we take for granted as dangers, such as hair dryers and appliances close to kitchen sinks, bath tubs, sinks, or toilets may start appearing. Radios and space heaters in the bathroom are a bad idea.

My parents lived in a house built in 1914. Some of the electric wiring had been updated, but the number of outlets didn't change. Mom would have a power cord plugged into an outlet. In the power cord would be another multiple outlet and so many cords plugged in. I would mention it to her and even tried changing the situation. The next time I came back, it was set up the same way again.

Another area of concern was their use of light bulbs. Their eyesight was diminished, so they started using 100 watt bulbs in 60 watt outlets. They would often plug in high amp things like a space heater into small wattage extension cords.

Keep an eye out for frayed electrical cords or other fire dangers. Look for scorch marks that could have been made by arcing electricity.

After my parents had moved to the Veterans Home, we were cleaning out their home. We found gasoline stored up high in the kitchen by the stove. It was marked "gasoline," but that didn't change the danger. A fire could have started on the stove, and spread to the cupboard where the gas was. Boom! The situation was ripe for an explosion!

ACCESS FOR EMERGENCY SERVICES

An ambulance ride could be a possibility as our parents age. Some older people I have known, pride themselves on having their furniture so close together that they can easily grab on to it as they walk by, "if they need to." That's all fine and dandy, but what I have seen is the walkways and hallways of their homes get clogged with these handy handholds/furniture. When the dreaded ambulance ride comes about, and the paramedics need to remove our seniors from their homes on a stretcher, it is a nightmare! A cane or a walker is always a better alternative to the "handholds." You may not have any luck changing their minds about this, until after the first ambulance trip.

WHEN DRIVING BECOMES AN ISSUE

"The one thing that unites all human beings,
regardless of age, gender, religion, economic
status or ethnic background, is that, deep
down inside, we ALL believe that we are
above average drivers."

~Dave Barry, 'Things That It Took Me 50 Years to
Learn'

In the United States, teenage drivers hold the number one spot for traffic accidents. Some would agree that most teenagers don't have the experience to call upon to prevent some types of accidents. They are more likely to drink and drive. The new threat to safe driving, in the age of technology, is texting while driving. There are many reasons teens are the number one age group for automobile-related accidents and deaths. Many states have special laws and curfews in an attempt to bring this statistic down.

The number two position for driver accidents goes to our senior population. The aging process is often accompanied by medical conditions and medications that can impair a person's ability to drive safely by affecting perception, judgment, or motor abilities.

One of the biggest hazards for any driver is not having a proper following distance to the car in front of them. There are factors of perception, reaction, and braking time of the vehicle on good or bad pavement. Seniors should have no less than two seconds' following distance at speeds below 30 mph on good pavement; better yet, make it three seconds. Remember, their reaction time can be slower than ours. Higher speeds require two or three times longer following distance depending on traffic and road conditions.

There are critical challenges in helping our aging parents recognize their changing abilities and adapt their driving practices appropriately. How do we recognize, identify, assess, and regulate impaired senior citizens, while sparing the competent ones?

When is it time for Mom and Dad to hang up the car keys and quit driving? Do we wait for an accident to let us know it's time for them to stop driving the four-wheeled beasts? If your parents are still driving, there are a few things you can watch out for to help them be safer drivers.

CAR SAFETY

To be a safe driver, no matter what our age, we must have a car sound enough to drive. When a person ages, they may not be driving as much. They may take their car out to drive to the store, or their doctor's appointment. When looking for the elusive "honey" of a used car, we salivate with anticipation at the "little old lady's" car which is in immaculate condition in the garage with extremely low mileage. What we don't like to see is our senior's car damaged beyond repair from a close encounter of the elderly kind.

Every senior driver is different. Some have their car serviced regularly by a mechanic whom they've trusted for years. They have their engine serviced, oil, fuses, and lights checked. Many elders have a newer, more expensive car. They show pride in ownership by keeping it clean. What I have found about car care is, the way a person is about their car when they are younger will continue into their senior years.

When I look at my youngest son's car, this is a frightening thought! Excuse me for making light of a serious subject. But I know that most people don't change unless they have a reason so motivating that they will go through the discomfort of making the change. Car care isn't usually a motivating topic to most people.

My parents kept a relatively clean car. When Mom's Alzheimer's was advancing, she became very obsessed about the cleanliness of the car. She talked about how the car was getting dirty in the garage. She fretted and stewed about it. She wasn't well enough to keep up with the constant upkeep she desired. Of course, what we focus on grows. The car became dustier. Thankfully, her car spent so much time in the garage, the battery ran down and it wasn't drivable without a battery recharge.

When it became evident that Mom had no business behind the wheel of a car, my husband stopped charging up the battery and making sure the car was roadworthy. We had peace of mind knowing that she couldn't get out and drive. Unfortunately, she had a AAA road service card. She would have them come out and pump up the battery for her trip to the store or the Farmers' Market. I always felt we were blessed by angels when she would lose her car keys! It was worth the huge amount of grief I would take from her accusations of stealing her keys.

If our senior is going to drive, it's important to keep their car maintained and in good working condition. Even though Mom would use her AAA card to have her battery pumped up when she shouldn't have been driving, it's a good idea for any driver to have this kind of card. We can't predict when a car malfunction will have us sitting on the side of the road waiting to be rescued.

I believe an area which gets overlooked at any age is dirty windows in cars. I know when I am driving around with dirt on the outside of my windows, visibility suffers. There's a film which gets on the inside of car windows from air conditioning coolant, heaters, and smoke. It can build up until it's like looking out of a cotton ball. Lights at night are distorted.

Headlights and taillights can become so dirty that visibility is a challenge. It isn't easy to spot someone stopping in front of us when we have dirty headlights. We can't count on someone stopping for us if they can't see our brake lights.

DRIVING ISSUES TO WATCH FOR

I'm sure you have all heard this joke about Mildred and Hazel.

> Two elderly women, Mildred and Hazel, were out driving in a large car, barely able to see over the dashboard.
>
> As they're driving along to the grocery store, they approach an intersection. The light is red, but Mildred just drives on through, not hesitating for a second. Bewildered, Hazel thinks to herself, *"I must be losing it. I could have sworn we just drove through a red light."*
>
> A few minutes later, they come up to another red light. Again, Mildred drives right on through. Hazel is alarmed, but is still not sure if she's imagining things. At the next intersection, however, Mildred drives through another red light, prompting Hazel to turn to her friend. *"Mildred, are you aware that we just ran through three red lights in a row?"*
>
> Mildred replies: *"You know, I noticed that too!"*
>
> Hazel, flabbergasted, stammers, *"You could have gotten us both killed!"*
>
> Mildred turns to her slowly and says, "Me?! I thought *you* were driving!"

People laugh at this joke. Obviously, Mildred and Hazel shouldn't be driving. It's so obvious that it sounds silly, which is why it makes a funny joke. We all know elderly driving issues aren't always this transparent or humorous.

The issue of our parents' ability to continue driving is a sensitive one. Their ability to drive is one of the last bastions of independence. It's paramount to their feeling, not only of independence, but of having control of their lives. I have always felt very respectful of their continued independence when it comes to driving. Of course, there's something else to consider. How safe are they and everyone around them?

Last summer, there was a hit and run accident near our home. A man on a bicycle was pedaling down the side of a two lane road. He was hit and knocked into the ditch alongside the road. The driver didn't stop. The bike rider was killed instantly. The search for the driver went on for a few days. Law enforcement finally found the driver. He was a man in his eighties. The elderly man didn't even know he had hit the biker! Sounds incredible, doesn't it? Newscasts are peppered with these sad events, stories of older people who mistake the gas pedal for the brake and run through Farmers' Markets, or a storefront, or other people's homes, killing and maiming others and often themselves.

When my father was at the end of his driving career, his ability to drive was punctuated by an accident. Thankfully, no one was hurt. He turned into the path of an oncoming car; both cars were totaled but no one was injured. Upon Mom's insistence, Dad's doctor reported it to the state and his license was revoked. Dad had to take the driver's written test many times, but he finally passed it. What eventually stopped his quest for his driver's license was when he couldn't pass the actual driving part of the test.

My husband, who had been a driver's education teacher for many years, worked with Dad to help him pass the driving test. Dad just couldn't remember to come to a complete stop at a stop sign. The Department of Transportation officer who rode with him, told him after three attempts that he wouldn't qualify to drive again. That was that and it left all the driving to Mom. A very scary deal, even when she was much younger!

RESTRICTIVE DRIVING

Many older people are disqualified from keeping their license because they can't pass the vision test. Many states will go out of their way to make some adjustments for them, if possible. Dad lost his peripheral vision. Before he lost his actual license, he had a restricted license which required he use larger mirrors on each side of his car.

One of the first restrictions to a license is usually a self-imposed desire to drive only during the daylight hours. Many people lose their night vision first and can still handle the responsibilities of limited daytime driving.

Before Mom2 voluntarily gave up her driver's license, she had gotten to the point where she only felt safe driving very short distances. She would go to the store, the pharmacy, or our house. All of these were not on busy roads and were very close to her apartment. To go farther than that seemed to make her very uneasy.

NOT SAFE TO DRIVE

A question which seems to plague all of us who have a senior driver parent is, "When is our parent not safe to drive anymore?" If this question rings true to you and you are questioning your parent's ability to drive, ride as a passenger with them. In this way, you can see how they handle their car. Here are a few things to watch for:

1.   When they are driving, or even as a passenger, are they confused about where they are?
2.   Does their car show signs of contact with other cars or their garage, such as foreign paint appearing on their car, or new dents and scratches?
3.   Do they have more than one medication that says on the warning label "can cause dizziness" or "don't operate a motor vehicle while using this medication"?
4.   Are they confused, or don't know how to respond at four way stops, or other intersections?
5.   Are they "stare driving," or not moving their eyes around looking for dangers?
6.   Are they not using their mirrors to see who is in the next lane or behind them?
7.   Are they making lane changes without signaling, or drifting into other lanes?
8.   When they change lanes, are they checking their mirrors for their blind spot?

9. Are they rolling through stops signs, or not coming to a complete stop at stop signs?
10. Are they in control of their car at all times?
11. Are they easily distracted?
12. Do they frequently hit curbs?
13. Are they having trouble merging into lanes or interstate traffic?
14. Do they use poor judgment making left turns?
15. Are they failing to follow traffic signs and signals?
16. Are other cars honking at them, often, wherever they go?
17. Are they staring at the end of the hood and not forward on the road?
18. Are they practicing safe driving techniques such as keeping eyes moving, leaving themselves an out, or making sure others see them?
19. Have they hit something recently where they had no idea what or whom they hit?
20. Are they making dangerous driving decisions when pulling the camper, boat, or trailer?
21. Are they following too close to the car ahead of them, not maintaining a proper distance?

If you are seeing these driving behaviors it's really time to think about discontinuing their driving. Which leads us to the next touchy subject....

HOW TO TAKE THE KEYS AWAY

Ouch! This can lead to WWIII. It can be a raw subject because do we really want our elder parent mad at us? The elder parent often feels like we are betraying them when we propose that it is time for them to stop driving. It can make us feel like such meanies!

What we need to consider is, how will we feel if we suspected it was time for our elder parent to hang up the keys and we didn't do anything about it. The elder parent, then, goes out and has a serious accident where they are killed. Maybe in this nightmare scenario someone else in the accident loses their life or is badly injured. How would we feel? Our gut feelings will start eating away at us if we don't take matters into our own hands. This subject won't win us any gold stars, but it is a necessity.

When Mom's license came up for renewal, she didn't realize it, and it expired. She had gone too long for it to be renewed without testing. Our state used to give six months, and now it has been moved to a year's grace period for a driver to renew their license from the date of expiration without having to take the driver's test.

I took her out to the Driver's License Bureau many times to try to pass the written exam. I had already started noticing signs of dementia, but rather than beat the bees' nest and cause a confrontation, I kept taking her out. I felt the driver's license bureau would be a better judge of her driving abilities. The final time she failed the written test, she exploded at me! She shouted that it was my fault she failed the test, and the fault of my sisters, who never visit. Yikes! My fears were confirmed. No rational thought there. I knew her mental faculties had slipped too far for safe driving.

Before Mom found out her license wasn't valid, she would

drive to the store or the Farmer's Market. When she came home, she would let Dad drive the car into the garage. The last time he drove into the garage, he hit the gas by mistake and ran the car clear through the garage. Their garage sits above the alley; the back of the garage is quite a drop down to this alley. He and the car ended up lodged against a telephone pole above and across the alley. Once again, he wasn't hurt, but the garage and the car were totaled.

Because Mom is a self-professed "in your face kinda gal," we didn't physically take her car keys. The car battery would run down and wouldn't start. When it was drivable, my husband would disable their car, which they wouldn't know about. I was paying their bills and I conveniently let the AAA membership lapse. This way, the AAA motor club wouldn't come out and jump the battery or reconnect the distributor cap. We made it next to impossible for her to drive, because she was the kind of person who would drive, even without a license. She believed it was her right because she was a senior!

My husband and I were always relieved when she would lose her car keys. She would blame us for taking them, but I always said it was her angels making sure she didn't strike out in the car and find disaster!

It may seem callous and unfeeling to skirt around the driving issue. I felt it was easier for all of us involved to not get confrontational about this situation.

Mom2 gave up her license without too much of a squeak. She has had an incident in her right eye where the major vein in her eye backed up and exploded blood into her retina, leaving her blind in this eye, with only slight peripheral blurred images. She is diabetic and her left eye is now having challenges on and off. Adding to the difficulty in her left eye, she is also experiencing the growth of cataracts. Her eye doctors are reluctant to remove the cataract in her left eye because it is her only source of vision.

She started customizing her white garage with torn-off boards and her red car had stripes of white; it was time to call it quits. She was having episodes of falling. She has numerous reasons for her dizziness: medications, low blood sugar, and low blood pressure. We took her car and her keys and moved them to our house. This stops the temptation to drive.

Every one of our parents is different. I have heard horror stories from one of my friends, whose father continues to drive even after the family has taken the keys. He knew he was having problems. The Department of Motor Vehicles had taken his license. He made duplicate keys and hid them from his family. Every day he gets out and goes for a drive, which is upsetting to his family. Thankfully, they live in the country where the traffic is less.

Sometimes this loss of independence is too much for someone with compromised mental health. One of my friends told me about his friend's father who drove into a pond and killed himself because his kids took his keys away. That may sound drastic, but when they see their days of independence leaving, they can panic.

I know how upset they can get, at first hand. My husband's dad had a heart attack and lost three fourths of his heart muscle. His doctor told him in the hospital that he couldn't continue to drive. My father-in-law decided at that moment that he didn't wish to live, and he was gone in less than a week.

When you're having to make the sad choice of taking their keys away, you can call your local hospital, or talk to your parent's doctor. They will know if there is a department at the hospital that could send a trained professional with your older driver, to see if they can function correctly behind the wheel. Ten years before my father lost his driving privileges for the last time, he had a stroke, and before he could drive again he had to drive for one of the hospital's professionals. At that time, he passed with flying colors. Because he was able to pass the occupational therapist's eagle eye in driving, we all felt better when he was behind the wheel.

Maybe you will be one of the lucky ones who can express your reservations about their continued driving and they will take heed and stop driving. But don't count on it! If you need additional information on talking with your elder parent about driving, AARP has a three-module course about this subject. Each module takes about 30 minutes to complete. The website for this is: http://www.aarp.org/home-garden/transportation/we_need_to_talk/. The Hartford has a little test to find out if your elder parent is a crash risk: http://hartfordauto.thehartford.com/Safe-Driving/Car-Safety/Older-Driver-Safety/crash-risk-assessment.shtml.

It may sound callous to take their car away from them. Please keep in mind, it's not just a matter of keeping them safe. It is about keeping other folks on the road safe, also. I always think, how would they feel if they caused an accident where they killed someone else? Maybe if someone had taken the elderly man's keys from him, the biker would still be alive to enjoy his family and his life.

HOSPITAL STAYS

"Acceptance of what has happened is the first step to overcoming the consequences of any misfortune."

~William James

I've had more than my fair share of my much-loved old people being in and out of the hospital. Mom was there so often the hospital admittance person called her a "frequent flier." Every time they are there it's stressful and concerning, whether it's an Emergency Room visit and they are then released to go home, or it's a hospital stay of many days. It often catches us unprepared. They can fall or have a serious illness that sends them to the Emergency Room with sirens and lights flashing.

Once they're there and it's been determined they will have to stay for a while, there's the school of thought that some-one should stay at the hospital with them day and night to make sure their loved one gets the best care. Some people put their faith and trust in the medical staff and leave and go home. It can be a puzzling situation. There isn't a right or wrong way to do it.

I've been in both situations. The decision to leave and go home for the night can be a tough one. Some of the things to consider are: Do we trust the hospital, nurses, and doctors? Is it going to be an extended stay of more than a few days? Is it an emergency or life and death issue that puts our loved one in the hospital?

I know one of the main things to watch out for is, staying at the hospital so long that the caregiver's health begins to deteriorate. Is it possible to spell off with someone else who is able to stay? If it isn't a life and death situation, can the caregiver leave it in the hands of the professional caregiver and feel okay with this decision? Only you can make the choice. Each time the elder is hospitalized might lead to a different decision.

Something that can cause major stress for the caregiver in a hospital situation is being caught unprepared and not having an organized plan of action. A plan of action may seem premature if our loved one hasn't had to go to the hospital. But as they get older and their health becomes more fragile, it will only be a matter of time.

I considered writing about the government programs that are available to help care for elderly parents. But the information out there is in a state of flux. The Affordable Care Act, also known as ObamaCare, is starting to be implemented and the biggest change to our health care system has only just begun. Social Security and Medicare will be impacted as well. I suggest the best way to stay current is to check the government websites for the most updated information.

HOW TO PREPARE FOR EMERGENCY ROOM VISITS

Emergency room visits are the ultimate stress-or! Our loved one is very ill or hurt, or we wouldn't be there. The stress factor is unavoidable to a certain degree. We don't want to see our person in need enough to be there, to begin with, but most often, the Emergency Room has long waits and uncomfortable chairs. I've sat for a week, one day, waiting. That sounds like a dichotomy, until you have been the person waiting.

I've found that the more prepared I am for the unexpected Emergency Room visit, the stress isn't quite as bad as when I was flying by the seat of my pants. Here are a few things to prepare ahead of time and keep in a safe location, perhaps in a backpack, where it's an easy grab as we fly out the door for our flashing-lights-and-siren tour of the city to the hospital.

1.   A file folder with copies of:
     a. the DPOA (durable power of attorney),
     b. copies of their living will if they have one.
     c. copies of the front and back of all their insurance cards (including supplemental insurance), Medicare card, Veterans identification card (if they have one), copy of their driver's license or picture ID of some kind.
2.   Keep up-to-date information in their file folder for all medications (including medications for skin such as cortisone, etc.), prescription and over the counter medications (including vitamins and supplements)

your elder is taking, with the dosages and frequency they take them. Be sure to know when they took the last dose of each medication and when they are due to take the next.

3. Also, in their folder, keep a list of all the hospitalizations and surgeries they have gone through. It is important to keep track of the dates and what each hospitalization was for. A brief medical history is important too. Questions like age of parents when they passed, what they passed from, and the same for your elder's siblings.

4. If they are on oxygen, note this and how many liters per hour they are on and how long they have been using it. If they are taking an ambulance ride, let the paramedic or EMT know this information and leave your elder's equipment at home. The paramedics will use their own oxygen equipment for the transport and the hospital will use the hospital's supply once your loved one has arrived. This is also true for wheelchairs, walkers, etc. This equipment is expensive and can get lost or misplaced in a hospital setting.

5. A list of their special dietary needs, allergies, and sensitivities.

6. Are you keeping a journal about your elder's health? It's a good idea to take your journal with you when you go.

7. A list of important phone numbers: doctors, loved ones, relatives, neighbors, home health care providers, pharmacy they use, pet sitter, etc. The phone numbers of those who need to be notified about the trip to the ER or notified if there will be a hospital stay. I keep the numbers in my phone, but

if you aren't a cell phone user, make sure there is an up-to-date list in your folder with all the other information.

I found my stress level decreased substantially when I had this information readily available. It helps the hospital professionals do their job, which equates to our senior getting better care.

5 TIPS ON MAKING THE HOSPITAL VISIT LESS TRAUMATIC

Aging senior citizens react completely differently than other groups of adults to changing medications, new and unknown surroundings, and stressful events. If your loved one is cognitively impaired or extremely ill, they can become very confused. I have always tried to stay with my beloved old person for at least 24 hours when they first get to the hospital. The hospital personnel understand how frightening and confusing it can be for an elderly person to be put in an unfamiliar place such as a hospital. My staying with my elder has always been met with appreciation.

Hospital workers are very appreciative of having the main caregiver present because that is the "go to person." We know our elderly loved one better than anyone. A word of caution: I found out the hard way that turning over the first 24-hour period to someone who isn't the main caregiver can be distressing for the elder, the stand-in caregiver, and the hospital staff. Why do I say such a strange thing?

Geriatric patients are at a higher risk after surgery. Sometimes, especially if they are diabetic, they can have longer recovery times. They often have heart issues or oxygenation problems. Their ability to bounce back quickly may be compromised by pre-existing conditions.

Mom2 was admitted to the hospital for a double mastectomy. My sister-in-law, who doesn't usually participate in doctor visits with her, insisted on staying with her in the hospital instead of me. I'm a laid-back person and I don't like to disagree with people. I'm not Mom2's daughter, only the daughter-in-law, and I thought it would be fine for her to stay with her Mom.

Her surgery went well. The problems began afterward. My sister-in-law wasn't familiar with Mom2's medications. My sister-in-law is a very "in charge" kind of personality. She has some medical training. I thought she was helpful to Mom2 because she would remind the nurses not to take blood pressures on Mom2's arm but instead, to take blood pressures on her leg. When Mom2 had the operation, the surgery recovery floor was full. Mom2 was put on a non-surgery floor. The nurses weren't accustomed to taking blood pressure on the leg. A surgery recovery nurse is used to it because after a mastectomy the arms aren't a good place to take it. My sister-in-law's reminders were helpful to the nurses and good for Mom2.

It's important to be an advocate for your hospitalized elder, not an obstacle. The drawback to her staying with Mom2 was that the nurses weren't as attentive as they should have been. Someone who seemed to have control of the situation was there all the time, to watch the patient.

She felt the nurses weren't attentive enough and she had to "do everything."

Another issue that derailed her was that she wasn't prepared at all for post-surgery delirium. I've been with my parents through numerous hospital stays and surgeries, and I understood that delirium can happen even with those who aren't cognitively challenged.

By the time I returned the next morning, my sister-in-law was in tears. She hadn't slept at all and she was worried sick about the delirium. Mom2 was disoriented and combative. She was saying things to her daughter that hurt her sensitive feelings, already ravaged by the lack of sleep. Knowing this wasn't usual behavior for Mom2, we sat down and started to unravel the puzzle of the delirium. The questions I asked were: What new medications were they giving her? What pain medications was she on? How much fluid were they dropping into her IV?

I immediately went to her nurse to get some questions answered. In Mom2's case, the delirium was being caused by the pain medication. Talking with the doctor, we were able to substitute a different medication, and the delirium cleared up in a little over 24 hours. Mom2 doesn't remember any of this time in the hospital.

I believe it may be important for the main caregiver to stay with the elder for at least 24 hours, especially if a cognitive issue such as dementia and Alzheimer's is involved. It is also important for the caregiver to take care of him- or herself. It's easy to get worn out staying in a hospital for days on end. Go home after the first 24 hours and rest. If it's important for someone to be with your senior at the hospital, let someone else be there. After all, that's another reason you've written everything down and have all your important documents in place.

As an experienced caregiver, I put together five points which can help make your elder's visit to the hospital a little less traumatic for both of you.

1.   Don't be afraid to ask questions. ANY TIME a medication is given, ask what it is and what it does. What are the side effects? WRITE IT DOWN!! Remember the note pad and pen from the list of things to have on hand at the hospital... this is another reason why. Even though you were very clear on allergies when your loved one was admitted, it doesn't mean accidents don't happen. Sometimes the doctor messes up and orders the wrong thing and the nurses don't catch it. You, the "go to person," might be the one who catches it, but only if you ask questions. Even if you annoy the hospital staff, wouldn't you rather annoy them than run the risk of having something preventable and bad happen to your elder? Don't think that could happen to you? The statistics about this are mind boggling!

2.   If you see something about your elder that has changed or isn't right as you know them to be, point it out. Keep pointing it out over and over again until someone listens. You know your care receiver better than they do. If you aren't getting any response to your repeated questions or what you perceive as an issue, go to see the Patient

Advocate in the hospital. His/her job is to help advocate between you and the hospital staff. Stick to it, as you could save your loved one's life.

3. ALWAYS read the tag on the IV bag. Mom2 is very allergic to penicillin. I want to make sure she isn't receiving penicillin in her IV drip as that would be life threatening to her. Make sure your elder's name is written on the bag. Wouldn't it be a disaster if your loved one got John Q Public's bag of chemotherapy and your loved one was in the hospital for something completely different than cancer? Yikes! But things like that do happen.

4. When test are being done, ask questions!!! What is the test for? What are the side effects? If surgery is going to be performed, why is it being done? When they take the patient away for a needed surgery, is the area marked on their body? Are the records correct on their chart? A surgery to remove a right big toe wouldn't be a success if they removed a leg instead, especially if it's the left leg!

Pay very close attention to what the doctor and the nurses are telling you. Again, WRITE IT DOWN! I have a very good memory, but hospitals can be stressful places. Stress can equal forgetfulness. I don't want to forget anything that has been told to me. I don't want my memory to have to sort out what's important and what's not. I write it all down. Before the doctor leaves the room, be sure you understand what was said to you. If you're having difficulty understanding a doctor's accent, ask someone to stay in the room with you and help you translate it. Nurses are very good at this because they deal with the doctor every day. If you don't understand a term they are using, ask what it means. Don't be afraid to ask them to explain more or repeat it. It doesn't matter what they think about you, it's your loved one that is important. It can all be done civilly. It's important to be polite.

5.   It's important to be patient and not lose your cool. The wheels in a hospital move slowly. Especially in a hospital's ER. Your elder may be sitting there longer waiting for help than someone who comes in from a bad car accident or is near death. But don't confuse patience with accepting things that aren't right. If you believe you are getting bad service, ask for a supervisor. The squeaky wheel does get the grease.

Recently, Mom2 was hospitalized for cellulitis, which is an infection from bacteria that attack the skin. It's a dangerous situation since our skin is the largest organ in our bodies. It's easy for cellulitis to spread to other organs or to the blood. It spread fast and we found Mom2 lying in bed, unable to move, incredibly sick. It was time for her first tour of the city with the lights and sirens flashing. She was one sick puppy.

She entered the Emergency Room with extremely low blood pressure from the infection. The ER staff took her off the Lasix diuretic she takes for her congestive heart failure because it was causing her pressure to go down even more.

The cellulitis spread to her blood and attacked her rotator cuff which had been damaged in a fall years ago, but never fixed. The Orthopedic doctor did a biopsy of her shoulder and ended up pulling three ounces of pus out of her shoulder. He then performed surgical repair to the rotator cuff. She had to have another procedure to check her pacemaker/defibrillator to make sure the leads and the pacemaker hadn't been compromised by the infection.

She was extremely ill. They started heavy-duty antibiotics. She started to get a little better until she had trouble breathing. Every breath was something she had to think about to do. She was panting and had to sit up. Knowing her health history, I raced down to the nurse's station to ask if they had been giving her the Lasix. Oops, they had forgotten to start it back up. She was in a major congestive heart failure attack!

The nurse came down to her room and gave her the Lasix by mouth. Fifteen minutes later, she was in more distress than before. Back down the hall I sprinted to tell her nurse she was even worse. He gave her Lasix in her IV and had the crash cart waiting in the hall. Very frightening experience. But wait! Scary experiences had only just begun!

The day after this major congestive heart failure episode, she was transferred to the Transitional Care Unit to start doing physical rehabilitation. She was put on oxygen and she was out of breath. She couldn't walk anywhere without panting. When I went up for a visit I saw her sitting in a chair with oxygen on and in distress. My first thought was the congestive heart failure was causing more problems. I checked her feet and legs and the edema was very pronounced. Her legs and feet were so swollen they looked like they would burst!

My husband and I were alarmed. We asked if her regular heart doctor had seen her. We were informed that they had to have a "consult" ordered to ask her heart doctor to come in to see her. She had technically been released from the hospital and was in the care of the Rehab Unit. We requested the consult and we were told the Rehab Unit had it under control. We insisted. The nurse practitioner came to see us and informed us, "You are the big sticks with her health care," and we could request whatever we wanted... but wait... they wouldn't order the consult because they had it under control.

I asked them how much she weighed. When they told me I was shocked! She had put on 25 pounds of water weight. She was 25 pounds heavier than the day she had come in, which was a week before. We requested a consult with her heart doctor again. They agreed to do a blood test to see if the enzyme for congestive heart failure was present. The next day when we came in they gave us the test results. Yes, it was present and very high. Wouldn't you think that would inspire them to honor our third request for a consult? No, not on their watch.

The next day, my husband and I were gunning for bear! We were going to visit her first and if the consult hadn't been ordered we were going to the hospital's Patient Advocate. The story now had changed to "she has pneumonia." They were going to have the Infectious Disease doctor give her additional antibiotics to treat it. As we were sitting in her room, the Infectious Disease doctor who had been treating her came into her room. He checked her out and told us she didn't have pneumonia. I showed him her feet and ankles which now looked like watermelons with grapes for toes. Her toes were literally purple! He pushed in on her foot and the indentation stayed after he removed his finger. He agreed she was in congestive heart failure, and said he would personally request the consult.

The heart doctor was able to come in that same day. He checked her out, ran some tests and told us she had congestive heart failure and blood clots in her lungs. He transferred her to the heart floor to begin treatment with additional blood thinners. Her hospital stay lasted one and a half months.

The lesson in my story is, I knew my elder's health better than the hospital did. I'm not meaning to be a braggadocio when I say that. I'm being factual. I could see what was going on and I wasn't going to take no for an answer. I became like a biting sow; I bit down and held on. Nothing was going to deter me from what I knew was right. If my husband and I hadn't been so verbal and insistent, we would have lost her. She wouldn't be with us today. Don't let anyone bully you into surrendering what you know is right.

MEDICATION CHALLENGES

As I mentioned before, elderly people don't react the same way to medications as younger people do. One thing I've found out the hard way is, some pain medications can put your elderly parent into la-la land that can actually have the appearance of dementia.

They can become confused, fitful, argumentative, have depressed vitals... and the list goes on. I can tell you from every one of Mom2's hospital stays, she didn't do well with post-surgery pain medication. She became extremely weak and disoriented. Her oxygenation dropped to 60% and she had to stay on oxygen.

She talks to people who aren't in the room. She has wild dreams. If your loved one seems to be reacting completely different from the way they usually act, check with the doctor. If you know your loved one isn't acting within the norms of their personality, you have the right to question the use of any medications. You also have the right to demand that your elder be taken off a medication that makes them loopy, and have them try something different.

Once again, it's very important to remember that you know your elder better than the doctor and hospital staff do. They see lots and lots of elderly people every year. Elderly people can have dementia and dementia-related actions. The hospital staff may not pick up on a change in behavior.

I've found that the hospitals in our area don't keep one nurse with a patient for the entire hospital visit. This means there could be a different nurse on every shift, every day. This can add to conditions being missed, especially cognitive ones.

The nurses get frustrated with Mom2 for not getting out of bed. Mom2 tells them to get lost, she isn't moving. Even when she tries to get up, she is weak and disoriented. She will seem to have lost her will to live. She can even be ultra-combative and mean-tempered. We get concerned about these changes in her personality. She can be feisty, but she isn't a mean and combative person. When she gets switched to a different pain medicine and starts to feel better, she turns back into her loving self.

Her oxygenation comes back up, and the oxygen mask can be taken off. She can get out of bed more easily and it seems to be the turning point in her hospital stays. She makes great strides getting her strength back and walking those halls!

REHABILITATION AFTER SURGERY, HOSPITAL VISIT, OR STROKE

Elderly people lose physical strength faster than a younger person. Surgeries and strokes can really knock them out. Elderly people want to be released to their home just like anyone else.

When a senior is in the hospital, Medicare is in the mix. Medicare is most retired people's first payer on their insurance. Medicare has certain rules and regulations. If a Medicare recipient can't walk a certain number of steps during their hospital stay, Medicare wants them released to a care facility for rehabilitation.

If an older person is living on their own, they have to be able to care for themselves. They will need to be able to dress, toilet, bathe, feed themselves, and be ambulatory for the situation they are in. If they aren't released to a care facility, they may qualify for in-home care. To qualify for in-home care, they can't go anywhere except to the doctor's office. They will need to qualify as a "shut-in."

This status qualifies them to have a nurse stop in and put their medications in their pill boxes, check their blood pressure, etc. As a shut-in, they may qualify for Medicare to pay for Meals-On-Wheels, a service where a volunteer drops off a daily meal for them. On Friday, they will receive two additional meals for the weekend days.

Medicare will continue to pay for the services until they can go out and join the world again. Once again, they can't go anywhere besides the doctor's office, if they want to qualify for Medicare help with their rehabilitation.

If they are sent to a Skilled Care facility (nursing home or physical rehab center) they will have to qualify to get out. I believe that if they are in the facility longer than 90 to 120 days, Medicare stops paying and they would need to qualify for Title 19, or have a long term care policy, or pay for this themselves. Please check the Medicare site when you need this information, as situations will change with implementation of ObamaCare. You can get more information at: http://www.medicare.gov/

Something to keep an eye out for: If they go to a rehab place like a care facility or a rehab location in a hospital, you will need to watch out for odd things which could blossom into a full-fledged medical crisis as it did with Mom2. The care facility or rehab location is focused on rehabilitation. They aren't watching for changes in the elder's medical condition and may be slow to react.

Transitional units are for physical therapy, period! They may not be up on other health care concerns such as cardiac, etc. They can dispense the patient's drugs and do the rudimentary exams; blood pressure checks, blood sugar monitoring, etc. They are very specialized in their approach. They are there to give the patient rehabilitation to return to their life as fully functioning as they were before the hospital visit or event which put them in the rehabilitation unit. They aren't used to dealing with other health issues.

WHEN UNCLE CHARLIE
COMES TO LIVE WITH US

*"All the mistakes I ever made were when I
wanted to say 'no' and said 'yes.'"*

~ Moss Hart

The Sixties were an interesting time. It was the era of the Beatles, Woodstock, free love and flower power! In many ways, it was the end of innocence. It was also the time period when the hit show *My Three Sons* was popular. It was one of my favorite shows. I laughed at the boys' antics, marveled at the befuddlement of their dad, Steve Douglas, and was enchanted by Uncle Charlie and all his grassroots wisdom. Uncle Charlie was everyone's perfect live-in grumpy house-keeper, confidant, and speaker of huge wisdom. He kept the family's clothes clean, the dinners made, and never failed to let you know when you were screwing up. Sadly, in this case, reality doesn't mirror Hollywood.

When it comes to the reality of dealing with our own Uncle Charlie or our aging parents, it would seem the logical thing to do would be to move them into our homes. But, unlike Uncle Charlie, who kept the Douglas family together, we bring our aging loved one into our home because it's become impossible for them to live independently. In years gone by this was easier to do as there was usually an adult who was a full-time homemaker. In today's world, this isn't as common.

In today's world, there are so many households where both adults work outside the home. Adult day care has sprung up to meet the need for supervision of our senior parents when the family is at work.

Adult day care can be a lot like a child's day care. The adult, like the child, is dropped off at the day care in the morning when everyone goes to work. They are picked up by a family member on their way home. At the adult day care facility, there are activities for the elder to do during the day. Often there are field trips and other outside activities.

The day care my father went to was amazing. The people who cared for him were loving and understanding. Just like a child's day care, the adult day care personnel are accredited, equipped, and prepared to take care of many of the same challenges as a child day care.

Since Dad was a veteran, when it came time that day care was needed, the Veterans Administration paid for two days a week for my Dad. Dad had an in-home social worker assigned to his case and she was able to do the paperwork with us. I can't express to you how helpful the VA has been to my family.

THINGS TO CONSIDER BEFORE SHARING YOUR HOME

When I was first married, my husband's Grandma Ruth was still living independently in her own home. Grandma Ruth was an absolute delight! She reminded me of my Grandma Bea. She had a great sense of humor. She had filled her life with many interesting experiences and told wonderful stories. I always thought she would have been a great author of children's books. She had been a teacher for a period of time, and a secretary to a prison Warden.

She had devoted her life to raising her only child, Mom2. One of the things she had been adamant about was her desire not to go into a nursing home. In her senior years after retirement, she volunteered a couple of days a week at a nursing home near her home. She made Mom2 pinky swear that she would never have to go to a care facility.

Mom2, being the dutiful daughter, brought her mother into her home when Grandma Ruth almost set her blouse on fire over the gas stove. This was just one of many telltale signs that Grandma Ruth's time in her own home was ending.

Mom2, being the dutiful daughter, didn't think twice about it. She moved Grandma Ruth into her home. It turned out to be an extremely difficult thing to do. It cost Mom2. She suffered caregiver burnout. Her health suffered from the strain of lifting Grandma on and off the commode many times a day.

She became increasingly aware of the constraints it put on her life. This was the time of her life when she and her husband should have been carefree to travel. They had raised their children, worked over 40 years, and were now retired.

During our lifetime with our parents, they may let us know they don't want to go to a care facility. To honor this desire, we consider bringing them into our own homes or moving in with them. This must be thought out very carefully. If you are considering cohabitation with your adult parent, there are a few things to think about. Let me play the devil's advocate and put forth a few things to contemplate.

What is your relationship with your elder parent right now and what has it been in the past?

Another way to word this question is: Why do we wish to move our elderly parent into our home? Does it have anything to do with guilt? Are we hoping our relationship with our parent will get better by moving them in?

If your relationship with your parent hasn't been good in the past, it won't get better by this arrangement. When their health begins to deteriorate, the demands on your time, finances, and patience go up exponentially!

When it comes to guilt, believe me, it won't get better if you move your parents into your home. You may not have the guilt of putting them into a care facility, but there will be a plethora of other things to feel guilty about. If your parent uses guilt to control you, it can get bad, fast!

There is a tremendous amount of stress involved as our elder's health deteriorates. Caregiver burnout is common, and is a heavy weight on the care giver. 63% of caregivers will pass away before the care receiver. That is a very horrifying statistic!

Living with all the responsibilities of an elder's care on a daily basis can be crippling to some people. When we care for children, there is a set amount of time when a child will be very dependent on their caregiver for every need. The older the child gets, the less dependent they are on their caregiver. In contrast, an elder care giving situation can last longer and be much more stressful. Elders don't grow up and get less dependent, they grow older and become more dependent as their health fails.

When I was a teenager, my best friend's grandmother moved in with her family. They had built a little apartment on the back of their home, especially for her. They seemed to get along fine with this arrangement. Grandma was just another member of the family around the table every night. When the children all moved away from home, and her grandmother was blessed with a very long life, my friend's mom became the main caregiver for her mother. It strained the marriage which was also suffering the stresses of an empty nest.

Will your family have enough room for family members and your elder parent to have their own space?

Households get very busy, especially if there are school-aged children around. An elderly parent who moves in with the family can feel irritated by the noise and activity levels. If there isn't enough room for personal and individual space, resentments can take on a life of their own. This can lead to an uncomfortable situation.

 Do you have a backup plan? I have heard the backup plan referred to as a "prenuptial type agreement for elder care."

Meaning, there is a backup plan which has been discussed with everyone involved, if the living-in arrangement doesn't work.

If they live a long life, their health will deteriorate. Is everyone in agreement as to what happens when the elder's health deteriorates to the point that the main care giver can't do it anymore?

Will there be someone home, or arrangements which can be made, to provide care all day and evening?

Taking care of our elderly parent can become an "every minute of every day" intensive situation. It may get to the stage where someone will need to be home with the elder at all times. If everyone works, or goes to school, there will need to be other arrangements made for when everyone is gone. An outside or professional caregiver may need to be hired. This can be taxing to a family's finances.

If the family wants to go on vacation, and Grandma and Grandpa aren't well enough to travel with them, an elder care sitter may need to be called in to stay with them.

If the children are at home with Grandma or Grandpa, will they expect the elders to be in charge, or will the children provide the care?

Not all children, of any age, are responsible enough to care for an elderly family member. It may work, perhaps, for short periods of time when the main caregiver has to run a quick errand or trip to the store.

Even with the most responsible children it can become cumbersome and they can grow to resent Grandma's and Grandpa's care needs. It's a situation to be carefully considered by all who would be involved.

How will it impact your marriage?

If one partner is up for it and the other is not, real problems can be brewing. Even strong marriages can feel the strain. A marriage that is already on shaky ground can be negatively affected by moving the elder in. I think it would be devastating to the elder if they thought their presence in your home was stressing the marriage.

Is the elder likely to insert themselves into the marriage or into your family disagreements? If their personality is the type to pick sides, it may add to family stresses.

How will this move impact your finances?

Caring for our elders can be a very expensive proposition. It might mean going down to one income. It may mean moving one person to a part-time income. Even if one person works from home, elder care can be very time consuming.

My personal experience has been that even though we didn't move our parents into our home, our incomes have been affected. My husband and I are both business owners. We have flexible schedules. Even with flexible schedules, we still miss time with our business in order to do the running, doctor visits, and everything else that comes into an elderly person's life.

Most elderly people have more than one doctor. I know my schedule can get very full when my beloved elderly people have doctor's appointments. When they are sick, it becomes even more hectic. My husband and I feel very blessed to have the flexibility in our careers that the other siblings don't have, but we pay the price in our finances.

What happens if our elderly responsibility gets sick or develops dementia or Alzheimer's disease? Would this still work?

People with dementia and Alzheimer's disease need constant care. The stress alone for the caregiver is huge. As the social worker for the dementia wing at the Iowa Veterans Home told my husband and me, "The difference between the elder staying at home or going to a care facility, is that in a care facility there are so many more caregivers to spread the challenges around."

No one wants to go to a nursing home. If it were a perfect world, we would live in our homes until the day we die, in perfect health until the end. I have heard so many people say their much loved elderly person wanted them to promise not to put them away in a nursing home. Sadly, that promise may not be the best for the older person, or for the family.

When we think of putting our loved one into a care facility, it can stir up such awful feelings of guilt and betrayal. When Mom developed dementia and it became impossible for her to live independently, I knew I couldn't take care of her in my home. I suffered feelings of guilt. She felt betrayed. She thought, if I really loved her, I would have her move in with me. As it turned out, moving to the care facility was the best thing for her. She is happy and our relationship has improved.

I suggest, if possible, seek out a professional who deals with elder care. Or, someone who has been down the road before in their own life. It's not something to decide on a whim. It'll take careful thought and prayer.

WHY IS DAD ACTING SO ODD?

"You're not the same as you were before.
You were much more... 'muchier'. You've lost
your 'muchness'."

~ The Mad Hatter (Alice in Wonderland)

Dementia and Alzheimer's rob our loved ones of many things, including their memories, and their ability to live in their own homes. Sometimes we can feel lost and sad when our loved one starts showing signs of dementia.

While people are living longer these days, dementia and other memory diseases are on the rise. 8.9 million adults (20% of adult caregivers) care for someone 50+ years old who has dementia.

Any caregiver who has given care for a person with dementia knows it is a time-consuming thing. The amount of time spent in the care giving role increases substantially as cognitive impairment worsens. To compare, the Family Caregivers Alliance reports that *"among people 70+ years old, those with no dementia receive an average of 4.6 hours per week of care, while those with mild dementia receive 13.1 hours of care weekly. For persons with severe dementia, hours of informal care received rise to 46.1 hours per week."*

The increase in cases may be linked to our longer lifespans. There are a number of other things that can cause dementia-like symptoms in our elderly.

One in four hospital admissions of the elderly are a direct result of medication issues, including, but not limited to, prescription drug interactions, as with Mom2 and her issue with Vicodin.

Adverse prescription drug interaction is so prevalent, that Consumer Reports on Health said, "Any new health problem in an older person should be considered drug induced until proven otherwise." The seniors in my family have numerous drugs they take daily. Mom2 takes 9 different prescriptions daily for her health issues. How do we really know what does what, when mixed with something else?

When I used to fill my parents' prescription boxes every two weeks, I found it can be very confusing just to fill the boxes correctly! So many different drugs needing to be taken at different times and in different amounts. Then there are the pills that need to be cut with the little cutter, that often cuts them incorrectly or shatters the pill altogether. It is mind numbing. It's no wonder they get messed up when filling their own daily medicine boxes.

There are other things which can cause dementia-like symptoms, too, such as: Parkinson's disease; the combined effect of weight loss/gain and medications; dehydration; vitamin B12 deficiency; falls and concussions; depression, and alcohol use. In Dad's case, his neurologist believes his dementia was caused by undiagnosed and untreated sleep apnea.

Dad's apnea was not found or treated until he was in his early 80s. By that time, his dementia was well on its way to robbing him of his ability to remember. The nightly change of using his CPAP machine was too much. He was never able to become accustomed to the mask or to using the machine. He was out of bed many times during the night to go to the bathroom because of his enlarged prostate, and could never remember to put the mask back on.

His neurologist told him the best thing he could do for himself to deal with his brain issues and his dementia would be to use his machine every night, and every time he took a nap.

Because of the apnea robbing his sleep, Dad naps every time he sits down. In fact, Dad can nap standing on his feet holding on to his walker. He is always very sleepy. His sleep study found that he startles awake from lack of oxygen 59 times an hour when he sleeps. That is almost once a minute!

Many people don't take sleep apnea seriously. They look at it as an inconvenience instead of the life threatening problem it can be. My brother-in-law had apnea for years and never sought treatment for it. Only when he suffered five strokes and had quadruple bypass surgery did he finally seek treatment. His treatment was medication and the use of a CPAP machine. Tragically, we lost him a year ago to heart disease at the young age of 58!

The causes of dementia are elusive. While we may, on occasion, find the cause of the dementia, it doesn't change the impact of it on our loved one.

SYMPTOMS OF DEMENTIA

Due to the nature of the condition, it's critical to get the dementia patient into a safe environment, which may mean taking them out of the home and into Skilled Care. They are dangerous to themselves because of their diminished mental faculties. Here are a few things to watch for, and examples from my life with Mom and Dad. The symptoms of dementia are:

Recent memory loss – Everyone forgets things for a while, but remembers them later. Dementia patients often forget things, and never remember them. They might ask the same question repeatedly, each time forgetting that you already answered it. They don't even remember they already asked the question.

Mom suffers from dementia. Her conversations and questions are repeated over and over. One of my sisters referred to it as her loop, because the conversation keeps looping over and over again.

It became very evident to my family, and to her in-home professional caregivers, that Mom couldn't take care of herself and remain in her home any longer. We had difficulty getting her doctor to make a referral for her to be seen by a psychologist. We needed the referral, so the visit could be covered by Medicare. She had been seeing the same doctor for many years; this doctor's specialty was geriatrics. I was at all of her appointments with this doctor. It became apparent to me the doctor wasn't interested, or wasn't equipped, to see Mom's deteriorating mental health.

Dad has had this diagnosis for many years due to a disease that causes plaque to form in the small capillaries in his brain. When the capillaries become full of plaque, that area is no longer receiving a blood supply and that portion of the brain dies and fills with water. To compound his health issues, he had also been diagnosed with Parkinson's.

Mom has always been the strong one. Her focus has always been on Dad. When he was taken out of the home to live at the Veterans Home, she became more agitated and confused. Her dementia became pronounced. She has always been a physically abusive person and she was getting even more combative and difficult to deal with. This was an extremely stressful time for my family and me.

Dad couldn't remain in their home. The Veterans Administration pulled the plug on his remaining there. Even with the many professional caregivers coming in every day to help, it wasn't enough to keep Dad up and moving. He was making frequent trips to the Emergency Room for falls, dehydration, and heart and stroke issues.

After Dad's last hospital stay, the Veterans Administration moved him to the Iowa Veterans Home. The social worker also visited Mom and told her why Dad was being moved there. She took Mom's application for residence at the Veterans Home at that time and we had to wait for it to be approved. While we waited, she became obsessed about looking for him. She thought he had gone for a walk and not come back. She thought he had been stolen in the middle of the night by my sisters and me. Then she invented strange stories of abduction by the government, etc. She was having such a serious short term memory loss that she couldn't remember from one minute to the next where he was. Even when we told her over and over again where he was, in less than five minutes she had forgotten. The stories were her way of dealing with not being able to remember.

She was extremely combative with me. Every day I worried about being attacked by her. It was obvious then that she wouldn't go to the Iowa Veterans Home on her own. She had forgotten she had put in her application to the IVH. She felt we were trying to "railroad" her into going. We needed to invoke the Durable Power of Attorney for Health Care directive. My parents had chosen my husband to be the POA when they did their wills. The key was getting her doctor to put in a referral to have a psychologist come over to evaluate her for cognitive impairment. If she was found to be cognitively impaired and couldn't make her own decisions, the Power of Attorney could be invoked.

I may be completely wrong on this. It is only my opinion, which added to $1.50 might get you a cup of coffee. I think that in some cases, some doctors are on the Medicare tit (I mean no offense with my language). They see the patient every three months for updates on their medications and it is steady money for the doctor. They see them this frequently so they can stay up to date with the elderly person's changing health needs. But some doctors don't want their patient to go to a nursing home, because it would end the patient's Medicare money coming in. Radical thinking, right?

I know there are some very good and dedicated geriatric doctors, and I mean no offense to them. But it is the only way I can describe how blatantly this doctor missed Mom's dementia.

I always went with Mom to the doctor's visit. Every time, the doctor would ask Mom the same question: How was she getting along with Dad? Every time, Mom would launch into what a creep my Dad was. How he irritated her. All the wrong things he would do. Every visit was a hostile tirade about Dad. There were never any cognitive questions such as what the date was, who was the president, what city did she live in. Absolutely nothing!! I would ask pointed questions of the doctor without trying to set Mom off on a tirade on me. The doctor would brush me off. I was exasperated! I tried talking to the nurse when Mom was in doing her blood work. I would be told to call and talk with the doctor about my concerns regarding her mental state and her safety in her home.

When I would call back to express my concerns with the doctor's nurse (I was never allowed to speak directly to the doctor except during Mom's visit), I was put off and told the doctor hadn't noticed any change in Mom. Really? Seriously?

As I said before, the dementia diagnosis was vital to invoking the Power of Attorney directive. As it stood, Mom was the POA for Dad and she was threatening to break him out of the Veterans Home (when she could remember where he was).

To get the referral, I finally had to tell the doctor's nurse that I was going to send a written complaint to the Medical Licensing Board about this doctor. Only then did I get the referral I needed.

The home health care company we were using for Mom's in-home care sent a psychologist/social worker out to her home to do the evaluation. Simple questions were asked such as, who is the president of the United States? What day is it? What year is it? The psychologist would have to tell Mom the answer, but when she was asked again five minutes later, she still didn't know the answers. When she went to the Veterans Home, they did a full workup on her and it was determined that she had Alzheimer's. They started her on the Alzheimer's drugs. The question in my mind is, could her Alzheimer's have been diagnosed earlier? Would starting her on the correct drugs have staved off her Alzheimer's longer?

At that time, I was unfamiliar with Alzheimer's. She and I were so focused on Dad and his well-being that I didn't pick up on her advancing cognitive issues. Now I know Alzheimer's doesn't just happen suddenly. It advances its way through the brain, slowly. I wish I had known and recognized these warning signs sooner in her.

Difficulty performing familiar tasks – Our loved one with dementia might cook a meal but forget to serve it. They might even forget cooking it.

The frightening thing about this point is, the person with dementia can forget they put the food on the stove. After Dad left the home, she couldn't even remember to eat.

Since Mom was a shut-in, she qualified for Meals-On-Wheels. They provided one meal a day for her.

I should have figured it out earlier. Even when Dad was still in the home, when I took meals over for her, which I did often, I was always concerned about her ability to reheat her leftovers.

Problems with language – People with dementia may forget simple words or use the wrong words, making it hard to understand what they want, causing an outburst of anger directed at the person they're talking to.

Our friend, whom my husband and I care for, has his own language. I know he understands most of what we say to him, but his responses to us are just a few catch phrases. He will say, "I have lots and lots of music. What am I going to do?"

His wife, who was living with him in the care facility, recently passed away. He began to say, "big ballrooms, what am I going to do?" Their only two sons passed away in the last ten years, leaving them without family to take care of them. He and his wife only have one sister each and both of their sisters are older than they are and live far away. After his wife passed, he would say, "one, two, three, four" (as he held up his fingers) and add, "now only one." We knew he was talking about his two boys and his wife who passed before him. Sometimes we can't figure out what he is talking about. We're still puzzling over the "big ballrooms."

Time and place disorientation – Someone suffering from dementia may get lost on their own street, forgetting how they got to a certain place and how to get back home.

They may not realize that time has gone by. They may be looking for a spouse, friend, or relative who has passed. They don't remember this fact because they may be locked into a different time period. When Mom had her evaluation, she thought it was 1964. I don't know what the significance of that particular date would be.

Poor judgment – Anyone might get distracted and forget to watch a child closely for a short time. Someone with dementia might forget about the child and just leave the house for the day.

Poor judgment is another reason it's dangerous for them to remain in the home. Dad would do strange things such as getting up on a chair in the dark to change a light bulb. Dad was always falling and can only walk with the help of his walker. Was he safe to be on the chair, by himself, in the dark? Absolutely not! I know I received a patch of gray hair over that one!

Problems with abstract thinking – Anyone might have trouble balancing a checkbook from time to time; dementia patients can forget what numbers are and how to use them.

Dad had always paid the bills. When his dementia worsened, he forgot to pay them. His squeaky clean credit rating, which he had always prided himself on, took a nosedive!

Services to the home were cut off. Mom took over the bill paying when she was 82 years old and had never paid a bill before in her life! I educated her on the subject of bill paying and balancing her checkbook, but it wasn't too long before she could no longer do it either. At that point in time, I took over the bill paying.

I highly recommend that the POA, or some other family member who is with them a lot, have his or her name put on the checking account. Mom wouldn't do this because she was increasingly paranoid and less trustful of every-one including me! She saw it as a loss of control, which was important to her.

Putting an authorized person on the checking account with them means, if a person slides into dementia or is sick for an extended length of time and can't pay the bills, the authorized person can step in and pay them.

Things like life insurance premiums can lapse if not paid in 30 days from the time they are due. Health insurance payments, if they aren't automatically coming out of the checking account, can lapse. Utilities can get shut off, etc.

Forgetting how to do simple things – One of the first things I noticed when my parents started their mental decline was their inability to do some very simple things, things they had been doing all their lives. Cracker and potato chip packages became unsolvable puzzles.

Something as simple as opening those packages frustrated them as they tried unsuccessfully to open them. Bubble pill packages take on an unfathomable ability to upset them as they attempt to get the dosage out. Some childproof medication lids and safety lighters become elder-proof.

Misplacing things – Someone with dementia may put things in the wrong places – dirty dishes in the microwave or a wristwatch in the cookie jar. Then they can't find them later.

This was common for Mom. Things turned up in the oddest places. She would always blame someone else for moving it or putting it in a strange place. For some reason, she blamed my daughter, who always had a close relationship with Mom. She would accuse her of sneaking over and stealing whatever she had lost.

Changes in mood – Everyone is moody occasionally, but someone with dementia may have fast mood swings, going from calm to tears to anger in just minutes.

It is so difficult to do, but crucial: the family shouldn't take offense with the mood changes. In my parents' situation, Mom's mood changes were directed at me. At times, it hurt my feelings. Many times, I had to take a break and distance myself from them. Often, it became very difficult for me to keep functioning in their lives.

When the mood changes and her anger were particularly bad, I would feel overwhelming sadness. Sometimes I would feel that the responsibility of caring for them was an oppressive weight to bear. I'd fall into deep depression. I felt like there was no end in sight! When someone's anger is directed at us, it's hard not to take it personally.

Personality changes – People with dementia may have drastic changes in personality, often becoming irritable, suspicious, fearful, or paranoid.

Drastic changes in their personality can go either way. Dad has always been a shy and reserved man. He has always had a lot of friends, but wasn't one to approach strangers. His dementia seemed to take away his reserve. He happily approached strangers, similar to how an extrovert would do. His shyness became a thing of the past.

Mom, on the other hand, became more suspicious and paranoid. I have always been her baby and someone she trusted completely. She became confused about things and would accuse me of making her life worse.

It is difficult to watch our parents change. When the change in behavior is directed at us it is heartbreaking!

Loss of initiative – Our loved one with dementia may become passive, not wanting to go places or see other people.

Dementia is a terrible condition. It can seem to wall a person off in their own little world. It's almost like they are fading away. It is often difficult for family to understand the changes in the one they love.

Many of the things they most loved to do, don't appeal to them anymore. They can lose their desire to see friends, and to go places they enjoyed in the past.

Inappropriate sexual behavior – People with dementia can start doing inappropriate sexual things that are completely foreign to them.

Dad was always a proper gentleman to everyone. He was not demonstrative with his affection. He wouldn't even kiss Mom in public or in front of us children.

When Dad's dementia reared its ugly head, Dad was uncharacteristically sexual. He liked to show parts of his body that shouldn't be shown in public. He began taking his clothes off and loved to be naked. He would touch himself in places inappropriate for public display. He would ask women, very nicely, if they would like to play with his private area.

To be truthful, it embarrassed me. I understand it's a sign of the disease, but that doesn't make it easier. I realized Dad wouldn't do those things in public if he were himself. He is now living on an all-male floor. He has to wear "onesies," a jumpsuit type of clothing that zips up the back, so he can't take it off by himself.

CARING FOR THE ALZHEIMER'S/ DEMENTIA PATIENT AT HOME

"I think it would be interesting if old people got anti-Alzheimer's disease where they slowly began to recover other people's lost memories."

~ George Carlin

When an elderly parent is diagnosed with Alzheimer's, some caregivers choose to bring their parent into their home. The gift of care giving can be one of the most loving and special things we can do for someone we love. It's a service which transcends this earth and is truly an extension of the Divine.

When someone makes this decision it should be done with eyes wide open. It should be done with the realization of how difficult and potentially overwhelming it can be. I didn't feel this was the correct option for me or my family. I'd made a promise to my husband and I knew Mom's personality and how it affected me. I chose to spend many hours and years in their home caring for them.

I've researched this extensively, so I can be a better resource for you if you make the decision to have them live with you. It isn't my place to encourage or discourage you from any decision you make about cohabitation with your loved one with dementia. It is your and your family's decision, alone.

My point is to provide information to help with your decision. I recommend that you get all the facts and make your decision fully informed. Realize it may not be an easy undertaking. Once you have gathered the facts, think and pray about it. It's a decision the whole family must make together, because it will impact every aspect of your life!

It can be rewarding and it can be frustrating. Many of us feel very responsible for our parents as they age. I know many children have given their mom or dad the promise that they won't "stick them in a nursing home to die."

They took good care of as we grew and matured. They changed our diapers when we were babies; shouldn't we do the same for them when they enter the winter of their lives?

This isn't a decision you can make with only your heart. Alzheimer's isn't, usually, a short term disease. It can go on for years. Even with the wonder drugs of today, they will continue to lose cognitive abilities and their health will deteriorate. Every day will bring new challenges. You'll be coping with constantly changing levels of abilities and new patterns of behaviors.

The things they could do all through their lives without thinking about it such as dressing, eating, toileting, etc., can become increasingly difficult to manage. Adding some common behaviors like wandering, sundowning, and hallucinations can become overwhelming to deal with.

People who are planners by nature, may have a leg up on care giving for an Alzheimer's parent. Not because the parent needs the plan, but because it can be a good coping mechanism for the caregiver. Much of it will be done by trial and error. Suggestions can be made, but if you embark on this adventure, it may feel like you are doing it by the seat of your pants.

I've found many of these suggestions to be true for me as I have been dealing with dementia and Alzheimer's with my parents. My husband and I also care for two dear friends of ours whose sons have passed. There was no one to care for them. When their health and mental capabilities diminished to the point where they could no longer take care of themselves, we stepped in. She has had numerous strokes and has been in a nursing facility for over seven years. Her husband, who was living independently, has been diagnosed with Alzheimer's. He has had to join her in the nursing home this past year. His mental abilities have deteriorated quickly.

When you are caring for an Alzheimer's parent in your home, study your day with them. See if you can develop a routine that makes things go more smoothly. Is there a pattern? Are there times of the day when they are less confused and more cooperative? Make the most of those times. Flexibility is the name of the game, as they will change and it may be necessary to change the routine as needed.

COMMUNICATION CAN BE FRUSTRATING

It can be challenging to communicate with them. They may not understand you and you might not understand what they are trying to tell you. Here are a few suggestions that may work in this situation.

1. Keep your tone reassuring and gentle. Use simple words and short sentences. Avoid baby talk. Refrain from talking about them as if they weren't present in the room.

2. When trying to communicate with them, minimize the distractions and the noise. Turn off the radio or television. This helps them focus on you and what you are saying.

3. Make good eye contact with them. Call them by name. It's important you make sure you have their attention before you start speaking to them.

4. It takes them longer to formulate responses. Give them that time and don't interrupt them.

5. If they are struggling to find the word for what they are trying to say, gently and lovingly see if you can provide the word for them.

6. Try to frame questions in a positive way. Being positive might keep things from taking a negative and combative turn for the worse.

7. Keep your mind open to their concerns, even if they are difficult to understand.

8. Be patient with them. If they told you the same thing five minutes ago, smile and respond as if it were the first time you heard it. Mom can ask me the same thing seven or eight times in a ten-minute conversation. I always act like it was the

first time I had heard it. What does it hurt to be patient and kind?

BATH TIME

Each Alzheimer's patient is different. When it comes to bathing this is very true. Some Alzheimer's patients have no problem with bathing. Others are very fearful. They may be afraid of the water or of slipping in the tub.

They may believe that they showered yesterday, when actually it was a week ago. When they begin the process, it's easy for them to become disoriented and fearful. They could have been fine about bathing last week, but this week is a whole different thing.

They could be fine last week with you assisting them, and this week they could say with anger that they can do it all themselves. Confusion and misunderstandings can lead to fear. This is when knowing that pattern of when they are most agreeable during the day can come in handy. Also, having a routine can help. Here are a few more suggestions that might help.

1.   Understand that bathing can be frightening and uncomfortable to them. Be respectful and calm.
2.   Communicate everything in advance with them. Let them do as much as possible themselves.
3.   Prepare in advance. Have everything laid out in the order you are going to use it in the bathroom before starting. Draw the bath or start the shower in advance before bringing them into the bathroom to have their bath.

4. Warm the room in advance. Have plenty of towels and their robe handy. Be sure to test the water beforehand. Not too hot, not too cold, but just right!

5. Never leave them alone in the bath.

6. Have safety equipment available for use: handrails (grab bars), shower/bath bench, a hand-held shower head, and non-skid bath mats.

7. As people age, their oil glands and sweat glands decrease in amounts. Their skin can get very dry and uncomfortable with daily bathing. It's probably not necessary for them to take a shower or bath every day. A sponge bath to clean the odor producing areas will probably work just fine on the days they don't take a shower or bath. Remember, don't give them "ass-facia." That means clean their face first, not the other way around. It's best to start at the top and work down.

8. Dry them off quickly, patting them dry. Remember, elderly skin can tear easily. Make sure to have the robe and slippers handy to bundle them up in. They get cold easily.

HELPING THEM DRESS

Dressing can be very challenging for an Alzheimer's patient. There are so many decisions and things to do. What to wear? How to put it on? The order in which clothes go on, and taking clothes off to put others on, can be very puzzling to them. Then there are those frustrating buttons and zippers. We can help them by minimizing the challenges as much as we can. This can help:

1. Don't forget their routine and the pattern we talked about before. Try having them get dressed the same time every day.

2. Encourage them to dress themselves as much as possible. Plan for extra time so they and you won't feel pressure or the need to rush.

3. Try limiting their selection of clothes to decrease the confusion. Keep a few outfits handy and the rest somewhere else. If they have a special outfit they like, buy a few of them. Remember, it isn't fashion week in New York. They don't have to match or be stylish!

4. Arrange the clothes they're going to wear by the order they should be put on. It may help to put the clothes in order from left to right. We are trained all our lives to do things this way – reading, handwriting, etc. This keeps them moving through the process with less confusion.

5. If they need help, try handing them the piece of clothing they are supposed to put on next. If they need prompting, do it in a gentle step-by-step way. One step and wait for completion, step two, etc.

6. Pick comfortable clothing for them, clothes that are easy to take off and put on. Keep the buttons, snaps, and zippers to a minimum. Elastic and Velcro are amazing for this! This keeps those frustrating clothes-related incidents to a minimum.

7. When they take their clothes off to put something else on, check for soil; remove soiled items from the room and put them to be laundered. This keeps the soiled clothes away so they don't put them on again another day.

HELPING ALZHEIMER'S ELDER EAT

It's a funny thing about Alzheimer's patients in regard to eating. Some seem to be hungrier than before, while others have to be encouraged to eat. When Mom was still living independently, she would forget to eat. She would make a Meals-On-Wheels dinner last all day. Needless to say, she got extremely skinny. She just forgot to eat.

Mom has always been tall and big-boned. She can carry 200 pounds easily without appearing to be overweight. When she got down to 160 pounds, she was gaunt. Her arms and legs looked like sticks. The weight loss began after her heart surgery but by the time Dad went to the Home, she was looking very underweight.

Since she has gone to live at the Veterans Home, she has put her weight back on. Her meals are structured and set up in a leisurely fashion so the residents have time to socialize with each other. She is happier and much healthier. When we are taking care of an Alzheimer's patient in our home, we can help them with their eating with these suggestions:

1. We can view mealtimes as an opportunity to socialize. We should be patient and avoid rushing. We should be vigilant for signs of confusion or anxiety.
2. Aim for quiet, calm, reassuring mealtime atmosphere. Limit the noises and distractions. Turn off the television.
3. Familiar routines are a comfort to them, but stay attuned to any changing needs they may have.

4.   Food choices are good, but limit them so as not to overwhelm the elder. Offer appealing foods that have familiar flavors, varied textures and different colors.

5.   In the early stages of Alzheimer's it's easy for them to overeat. With an Alzheimer's patient it's best to serve small portions or several small meals throughout the day. Make finger foods, healthy snacks, and shakes available. Mom enjoyed Ensure drinks, which are very nutritious and easy to drink.

6.   Choose foods and eating utensils that are easy for them to use, encouraging independence. Bowls instead of plates, built-up silverware, straws, or cups with lids to make drinking easier.

7.   Encourage them to drink plenty of liquids throughout their day to avoid dehydration.

8.   As Alzheimer's progresses, it's much easier for them to choke on food due to chewing and swallowing problems. Sticky foods such as peanut butter should be avoided. Watch for the signs.

9.   Get them to the dentist for their regular checkups. Keep them going on their twice daily brushing. Oral health is very important for their overall health. Gum disease and rotting teeth cause heart problems and other infections which can turn life threatening.

ACTIVITIES

Alzheimer's patients are more comfortable with doing an activity they already know how to do. Obviously, it's harder to teach them something they have never done before than to keep up with something they already know how to do. If they aren't a puzzle person, they won't have success with them after they have Alzheimer's.

Don't expect too much. Simple activities are the best. They may need some assistance getting started. It works well to break down the activity into smaller, more manageable and understandable steps. When they accomplish even the smallest thing, praise them for it.

Keep in mind their schedule and when they seem to have more patience for activities. If they seem to get frustrated or agitated, it's time to put it away for tomorrow. Distract them with something else.

Help them feel a part of the family team. If they are able to cook, let them. Keep a watchful eye. They can do things to help such as setting the table, clearing up after the meal, helping wash the dishes and putting them away. This helps them to maintain their functional skills, gives them a better feeling of controlling their situation, and it helps you out.

Take advantage of adult day care. It's a wonderful time for them to socialize and do activities at their level of competence. It also gives you a respite to do something that enriches you, or to just take a rest from care giving.

INCONTINENCE WITH ALZHEIMER'S

One of the troubling side effects for the Alzheimer's patient and care giver is incontinence of bowel and bladder. The invention of throw-away undergarments such as Depends has been a huge boost to people who have incontinence issues. Mom2 refers to them as her diapers – a humorous way to look at something that some people see as embarrassing. Disposable undergarments have come a long way in absorbency and how they look under outerwear like slacks. They are a lifesaver for dribbling problems or any incontinence issues. Even though incontinence is typical of Alzheimer's patients, it could also be the result of a physical illness. It should be checked out thoroughly by their physician.

Many tips for helping our Alzheimer's elder are similar to potty training a toddler. We won't be "potty training" them. I mean no offense to anyone in using that analogy. It helped me to understand the process behind the tips.

Have a routine – Here's another situation where being organized and having a routine helps both the elder and the care giver. Take the person to the bathroom every three hours or so during the day. Don't wait for the person to let you know or ask for help to use the bathroom.

Look for signs they need to use the bathroom – They can pull at their clothes, seem agitated and restless. When they show these signs, it's time to hotfoot it to the bathroom with them.

Be understanding when they have accidents – Just like our blessed little potty training toddlers. If we freak out and get upset with them, it only increases the incidents. They are probably trying to do their best not to have accidents and can use our understanding. If you feel that they are doing it on purpose, like our toddlers, they could be doing it for the attention. Sometimes, negative attention is getting them what they want. The best way to be is calm and understanding, especially if they are upset themselves. Keeping track of when the accidents typically happen can give us insight into helping prevent them.

Preventing night time accidents – Limiting their fluid intake at night can help, especially caffeinated drinks such as coffee, tea, and soda.

Planning for outings – When taking them out and about, it's always good to be in the know about the location of the bathrooms. Keeping the person in simple, easy to remove clothing can help. Packing a bag with a change of clothing may be prudent.

SLEEPING ISSUES

When Dad was living at home, this was a very troubling situation, which I knew nothing about at the time. This is called "sundowning" or "Sundowners" syndrome. Dad would be increasingly agitated at night. He would wander around all night long. He would wander into Mom's bedroom and wake her up. I thought he did this because he had always worked the night shift at the paper. It made sense to me that he might revert back to this nocturnal behavior.

What I found out later is that it is very common in Alzheimer's patients. It's a dangerous situation for the patient and the care giver. They can wander around at night getting into all kinds of things because the care giver is sleeping and thus they are not being supervised.

It's helpful, again, to have a routine set up – something that stays as much the same as possible, night after night. If you have moved them into your home, providing some of the things they are used to doing at their home at night can be helpful. The routine should have things like putting their pajamas on and brushing their teeth in the same order at the same time every night.

Getting the Alzheimer's patient to go to bed after sundown can be trying. They would like to stay up and wander around until dawn. Here are a few tips on things that might help curb this behavior.

Encourage exercise during the day and limit day time napping – They will still need to get some daytime rest because "sundowning" can be exacerbated by fatigue, which increases the chances for evening restlessness.

Dad was a walker. He enjoyed walking all over the neighborhood. He had friends to visit everywhere. He was able to continue his walks for most of the time he was living at home. We had him take his cell phone along, with all his information in it. I don't know how safe it was for him to continue his pattern of walking, but it seemed he started with the "sundowning" when he was unable to take his walks.

As he was a walker, it was hard for us to keep him from leaving and going for his walks when it became dangerous for him to be out alone.

Because Dad had severe apnea, it was almost impossible to keep him awake during the day. He would sleep wherever he was. He could be in mid-conversation and he would doze off.

Limit the intake of caffeinated drinks in the afternoon – Dad loved coffee. He could drink it all day long. We started replacing his coffee with a half-and-half blend of regular and decaffeinated coffee. We had tried to switch him to all-decaf right away, but he could tell the difference and hated it. We switched to the blend and he didn't seem to notice. After a while, we took out more and more of the regular coffee until he was drinking 100% decaffeinated.

Schedule physically demanding activities earlier in the day – Bathing should be done in the morning. Even when scheduling meal times, the heaviest meal should be served at midday. I know, when a professional caregiver is giving the baths, it may be difficult to get it into their schedule in the morning. With my parents, the caregiver would come in to bathe Dad in the morning and she would do some light housekeeping in the afternoons.

Keep evenings peaceful and low key – Some lower lights, soothing music, and keeping loud noises to a minimum can help.

Bedtime should be consistent and routine – Again, being organized and having a routine can help here. Getting into the habit of brushing teeth every night at a certain time, putting their pajamas on at the same time every night, etc., is helpful.

Use night lights in the bedroom, hallway, and bathrooms – Getting up in the night can be very disorienting.

Getting disoriented can be frightening for someone with Alzheimer's. Heck, I like to have a night light to navigate by if I have to get up to use the restroom in the night!

Create a "safe place" for your elder to sleep – You need your sleep too! Their safe place should be someplace they can wander without having problems. This will add greatly to your peace of mind and to a good night's sleep!

HALLUCINATIONS AND PARANOIA

Hallucinations and paranoia can be very unsettling. According to the Alzheimer's Association of America, 25% of those afflicted with this disease will suffer from them. They define these hallucinations as "false perceptions of objects or events" involving the senses, caused by the changes in the brain resulting from the disease. Sometimes they can be a sign of a physical illness or medication, such as Mom2 had in the hospital after her mastectomy and her issue with pain meds. A medication can trigger hallucinations and it's always wise to let the doctor know when they start to happen. Getting a proper diagnosis is important.

In my case, Mom had many hallucinations and they were unsettling because they were so personal at times. For instance, Mom would swear that our daughter, who had always been her favorite grandchild, was coming into her home and stealing little things – like a pair of scissors, her dog grooming clippers, jewelry, or anything she misplaced. She swore up and down that she had seen our daughter come into her home and steal whatever she was missing.

Our daughter wasn't concerned. She knew she hadn't done it and she knew that Grandma was ill. It was more upsetting to me, for some reason. I don't know exactly why. I think it's because I'm a ferociously loyal mother. I always want to protect my cubs. I kept my cool, but I fumed on the inside!

Her scissors, or whatever she claimed was stolen, would show up underneath some items of clothing or in the wrong place. At that point, she would claim that our daughter had sneaked back into the house and put them there so Grandma couldn't find them.

Arguing with an Alzheimer's patient never goes well. It didn't in my case, for sure! She would get even more upset and combative. What worked best was to take my daughter's approach and let it go. Don't take it personally. Change the subject. Take them outside or to another room as a change of scenery and to help them get off the subject.

I had to work on myself to not let it bother me... to just let it go. It helped to distract her with another subject. Her memory is short and changing the subject worked many times.

Some elderly people with dementia and Alzheimer's get fixated in believing that someone is trying to murder them or poison them. They can become very frightened by their delusion and hallucinations. Comfort and reassure them. Reaffirm that you are there for them. "I'm here, I'll protect you." Don't pooh-pooh them as though it doesn't matter. It matters to them and these are real events in their minds. Express a simple, "I understand you are worried/ concerned." A gentle pat to return their attention to you can help reduce the hallucination.

When a violent television show comes on, turn it off or change the channel. They can have a hard time distinguishing between fantasy and reality. If they have hallucinations or paranoia about strangers in their room, covering the mirrors might help. Do some investigation about strange noises and phantom objects that could be a result of an air conditioner or furnace kicking on, or the light coming through their windows that has bounced off the neighbor's house, creating strange light patterns in their room.

Sometimes the hallucination isn't bothersome to the elder. Their hallucination could be the result of a memory. They could be seeing their long deceased mother or friend. They could have lengthy conversations with their hallucination, and they may be comforted by this. They could get some resolution to a situation that has been troubling them for some time. In these cases, the caregiver is usually more upset than the elder. The caregiver may feel put off by these hallucinations because they remind us that our loved one is having cognitive issues. But does it hurt for them to have conversations with the long deceased mother or best friend?

Make sure, always, to have objects they could use to hurt themselves or anyone else unavailable. It only takes a second for a delusion or hallucination to become deadly if they have items accessible that they could use to inflict harm on themselves or others.

The best thing to do is to discuss this with their doctor. If this is something new and they haven't been diagnosed with Alzheimer's or dementia, it could be an early sign of it starting. It could be due to the medication they are taking. The doctor can puzzle this out and proceed with steps to alleviate it.

Hallucinations can become so severe that a person with Alzheimer's can't take care of themselves. They may even progress to the point that they will need 24-hour care in a facility that specializes in Alzheimer's and dementia care. If this becomes the case with your loved one, don't feel guilty.

In my case, I used it as a valuable lesson in life. I had to learn not to let it upset me. The relationship I had with my parents whom I love has changed. Only I control the way I react to them and to life's situations. One of the beautiful things about lessons in life, even if they are painful, is that we can choose to find the precious gem in the mud and clay of adversity. We can choose by our attitude how we see and react to these things.

WANDERING

I was one of the luckier caregivers when it came to wandering. Dad, being the avid walker, always wanted to take a walk. He had lived in the same house and neighborhood for over fifty years. He didn't become confused when he was out walking. By the time his dementia was severe, his heart and his health were challenging enough that he could only walk around the block. Our problem was, as his dementia progressed, he wanted to go walking at all times of the night and day.

Right before he moved to the IVH, he started going out in the nighttime to "pull weeds behind the garage." It was difficult to keep him inside. It was only a matter of time before he would have gotten lost.

An Alzheimer's patient should always have identification on them, such as a wallet, cell phone with all their information listed, or a bracelet. Dad hated any kind of jewelry and wouldn't wear it, but he would carry a cell phone. Once, when he went out for his unscheduled walk, he fell. He had his cell phone on him, which had his home number listed as "Home" and my number listed as "emergency." A caring individual stopped and was able to get in touch with Mom and me with our numbers listed as such.

It only takes a second for them to sneak out and get lost – in either warm or cold weather. We've all heard the stories of an elderly person with Alzheimer's sneaking out of the house, becoming lost, and freezing to death in the cold or suffering from heat stroke on a hot summer day. Whatever form of identification you choose to use should always have their name, address, their caregiver's name and phone number, any medications they are on, and that they have Alzheimer's. It's optimal to have identification on them that can't easily be removed.

There is a program called the Alzheimer's Association Safe Return program. It isn't available in every area, but it is easy to check into and enroll your senior. Another national program is the Project Lifesaver, which works hand in hand with trained public safety agencies to find those who wander. A call to your law enforcement agencies can let you know if one is available in your area.

Introduce yourself and your Alzheimer's care receiver to your neighbors, before they start wandering. Let them know that your loved one has a tendency to wander. Neighbors can be a great help.

Always have a current picture of your loved one that can be accessed quickly, in case they wander off and law enforcement has to be called.

Keep doors and windows locked at all times. It might be time for a keyed deadbolt or an additional lock up high or down low on the door. Getting rid of the lock they are used to and replacing it can help.

"Announcing" systems are available. This is a system that will chime or verbalize when a door opens or is ajar.

It can be very frightening when our loved one with Alzheimer's starts wandering. It can happen as quickly as a wave hitting a beach. Just because they haven't wandered in the past, doesn't mean they won't tomorrow. Preparation in advance is important.

HOME SAFETY FOR THE ALZHEIMER'S PATIENT

Earlier, I wrote about home safety for our elderly loved ones. When they have Alzheimer's it should be looked at with a fresh set of eyes. Creating a safe home environment can go beyond what we would do to keep our elder safe. A preconceived, thought-out plan and precautions can prevent many stressful and dangerous situations.

Letting our neighbors and law enforcement know our loved one has Alzheimer's can be a good place to start. Introduce our elder to them in a safe setting with you by their side.

Reviewing safety measures once a month can be helpful. A written record of what needs to be changed or what has recently been changed will help keep you organized. When we entrench ourselves in our care giving, things will pop up, and writing them down will keep us organized.

Securing the yard with fencing and a locked gate is a good safety precaution. Install locks on doors and windows. It's not uncommon for an Alzheimer's patient to sneak out through an unlocked window or door and become lost.

Put all potentially dangerous items, inside and outside of the house, away and locked up.

Be vigilant on kitchen safety. Watch for things such as leaving the stove on after cooking. It may be time for a device to be installed that will shut off the stove automatically to prevent fires.

Keep the house free of clutter that can trip our loved one. This includes removing throw rugs and extension cords – anything that could turn into a fall.

Label all medications and keep them locked up and away from our loved one. Mom got to the point where she didn't remember whether she had taken her medication and would take too much or forget to take it. When she was younger, she was always one who would self- medicate. She became worse about it when her Alzheimer's progressed.

Remove locks on bathroom doors to prevent them from accidentally locking themselves in. Use childproof latches on kitchen cabinets and anywhere cleaning supplies or other chemicals are kept.

ALZHEIMER'S + DRIVING = DEADLY

Age can be a hindrance to an elder's driving skills. Alzheimer's is devastating to those skills. It's difficult to make the decision to take away the keys. To not make the decision endangers not only them, but everyone else on the road.

A driver with Alzheimer's can struggle with the ability to prioritize visual cues. A simple thing that wouldn't distract a normal driver can steal the attention of the Alzheimer's driver. Movements such as children playing in a fenced yard can draw their attention away and they don't notice other things like brake lights or stop light changes.

They have a rapid decline in their judgment skills. A car can look further away than it really is. They can cross the center line and not realize it. They think more slowly and are unable to make quick decisions that could save their life and the lives of those around them.

Refer back to the section on when it's time to take their keys away.

DOCTOR AND DENTIST APPOINTMENTS

Doctor and dentist visits are an important part of our Alzheimer's patient's life. Catching medical conditions early is vital to their care. The doctor has the opportunity to talk with the patient and discuss changing issues with the caregiver.

The doctor's or dentist's office can be a scary place for our elder. Advance planning on our part can help the visits go more smoothly. We can schedule them for the time of day that is best for our elder, when they are more likely to have an easier time interacting with others. Before Mom and Dad went to the Veterans Home, I would try to schedule their professional health care visits when the wait would be shorter and the waiting room less crowded. Mom would get more agitated if we were sitting side by side with strangers.

One suggestion that others have found works for them, especially with the dentist staff who may not see many Alzheimer's patients, is to let them know in advance that your person may be confused. Let them know what can help the visit go more smoothly.

Another way to cut down on the confusion factor is to wait to tell your loved one about the appointment until shortly before it's time to go. This lessens their chance of getting worked up about it. It helps to stay positive and matter-of-fact about it.

It helps to keep them occupied if there is a wait by bringing an activity they can enjoy to keep them busy. Mom always responded well to having a little snack while we waited. I would bring some granola bars or a piece of fruit. She enjoyed having a bottle of water to drink because her water pill always left her feeling thirsty.

Always carry an updated medical history and medication list with you for these visits. The doctor will need a current list, especially if your loved one sees more than one doctor, where they could be prescribed other medications. Each doctor needs to be kept informed of any other visits and what was done and what happened at those visits.

In our city, there are two medical professional groups. Their computers don't communicate with each other. Blood work, etc., isn't shared, except by me. I've asked them to fax the other doctor the information, but it doesn't often happen. When possible, it would be nice to stay in the same care association so this information can be shared without having to manually take it. The changes in Medicare and the new health care laws coming into effect will probably make communications easier.

If possible, it's handy to have an additional person who can go with you to keep your loved one busy in another room while you speak to the doctor.

VISITS FROM FAMILY AND FRIENDS

I found, in my family situation, that many of our family members have a disturbing attitude about visiting my parents. Their attitude is, "They won't remember I visited, so why bother." That attitude left me isolated in my care giving.

I think the human interaction is important to Alzheimer's patients because it keeps a connection to others. Even though my siblings didn't feel that my parents know if they have had a visit, I know it's important to my parents. Only one of my sisters visits with any regularity. Another sister, after my prompting, would call regularly. My other sister didn't call or visit for years.

Many people are uncomfortable with Alzheimer's patients. The repeated questions can make the visitor cranky and irritable. They get frustrated and can be short and dismissive with their Alzheimer's loved one. With a little coaching, they can realize that their loved one isn't saying things over and over again to upset them or the family. The person with Alzheimer's honestly doesn't remember asking the question or hearing the answer before.

Mom repeats herself over and over. She can ask the same question many times in the span of ten minutes. It doesn't do any good to snap at her and tell her "You already asked me that five times before!" I always smile and answer her question as if it is the first time she asked. She can't help it, and to treat her with irritation and annoyance is mean and shows ignorance of the disease. If she gets on a loop, I attempt to redirect the conversation. She may go back to it and ask again, but so be it. I choose to be loving and supportive.

Visiting someone with Alzheimer's can have other frustrations. Friends and relatives will be looking to the caregiver for direction on handling visits. Most Alzheimer's patients have their own times of day when they are more alert and coherent. They are at their best during this time of day. It's a good idea to plan the visits during those times.

I find it helpful to bring an activity to engage the loved one. I have found pictures are a great way to connect. They may not recognize those in the picture, but they enjoy looking at them and being reminded about each person.

Sometimes, this helps bring to their mind memories from the past. When Dad's dementia started, he clung to pictures and stories from his past. Mom enjoys seeing pictures of the family as they are now. She doesn't recognize the people but it makes her smile to look at them. Some days aren't good for pictures or an activity. On those days, we skip them.

Some visitors need to be reminded to stay calm and quiet. Loud voices and excitement can make the Alzheimer's patient agitated or irritable. Speaking to them as if they were a child is another way to upset them.

We should respect their personal space and not get too close. When I want to hug Mom or Dad I always say something like, "I'd like to give you a hug and kiss." Grabbing them for a hug and kiss too abruptly can frighten them. When you announce your intentions, you can see if they are responding favorably to the idea or leaning away from you.

Establishing eye contact and calling them by name is a good way to get their attention. Doing this not only gets their attention, but everyone likes the connection of hearing their name and looking into a loving person's eyes. If they don't seem to recognize you, kindly remind them who you are. When I go into Mom's room to visit, I always make eye contact and tell her who I am. She may recognize me before I say who I am, but sometimes she doesn't. She always brightens up when I tell her who I am.

When we visit with our children, I remind them ahead of time to do this. I know it makes Mom feel better to know right upfront who they are. Otherwise, she knows they are a grandchild, but most of the time she doesn't know exactly who. Don't feel bad if they don't recognize you, just gently remind them. Above all, remember, don't take it personally. It doesn't mean they don't love you. They are just confused at that moment. Just breathe and smile.

If the person seems to be confused, don't argue with them. One of the things I see people do with Alzheimer's patients is argue about details. This is upsetting to everyone. Who really cares if they don't have their facts straight? They may not remember five minutes later. Is it so important to have the facts straight as you see them? Lighten up, let it go. It's better to read their energy on how they are feeling about something. Wouldn't it be better to let it go and just enjoy seeing them smile when they tell you a story about something you know isn't the way they remember it. Isn't one of the reasons for visiting them to lighten their day and make them feel loved for however long you can?

Save the tears for later when you aren't in their presence. Dad doesn't remember me very often when I visit. Even when I use the above tactics it just doesn't seem to happen most days. When that is the case, I know it's not a good day to visit. We keep our visit short and upbeat. Seeing him like that always makes me sad and I miss who he used to be. I refrain from crying in his presence because I know it's confusing for him to see anyone cry. After I leave, I give myself a little time for grief and tears. Then I remind myself, next time he may know us.

It's hard to keep visiting Dad when he doesn't know who I am or that I'm even there. I continue to go because I love him. Sometimes he does know me and I cherish those visits. They are few but so very special!

CHOOSING A CARE FACILITY

"Put a good person in a bad system, and the system will win every time."

~ W. Edwards Deming

There is a bumper sticker you may have seen. It says, "Be kind to your children (they pick out your nursing home)." A little humor for a serious subject.

Baby boomers, we all know, are the largest age group of people ever. Every industry they come in contact with and whose services they need has exploded! Back in the day when the baby boomers were little babies, companies like Gerber exploded in growth. The boomers got a little older and companies like Mattel and Hasbro grew to be huge companies.

Later, as the boomers hit the teenage years, fast food restaurants began their meteoric rise to prominence! It only makes sense now, since the boomers are aging, that retirement communities, assisted living, and nursing homes will be hot properties.

ASSISTED LIVING VERSUS NURSING HOME CARE

Many people become confused about the differences

between assisted living and nursing homes. In order to make a good choice for living arrangements for our senior loved one, it is important to understand the differences. They are many.

Assisted living is a much more independent lifestyle. The candidates for assisted living may need help with daily activities such as bathing, dressing, grooming, and preparing food. They could even use some help with medications. They might need some help with preparing their pill boxes or reminding them to take their pills.

In an assisted living situation, seniors usually have better mobility. Better mobility can lead to better socialization activities. They can still make their own decisions about their daily life. At this stage of their elderly life, they would find a nursing home too restrictive and a nightmare to live in.

Assisted living situations can have limited medical care available. They may or may not have access to a nurse or doctor 24 hours a day. It depends on the assisted living establishment. Their residents need to be in fairly good health, both mentally and physically, to qualify for assisted living.

Assisted living is a viable alternative for ambulatory and mentally sharp seniors who would like to move out of their bigger homes into a more manageable apartment. The assisted living elderly resident lives more independently than a nursing home resident. It is apartment living with light housekeeping and meals provided. There is someone who could come to their aid if they should need assistance.

Nursing homes help with all activities and medications. Privacy is more limited. In many nursing homes, residents share rooms; there can be two or three people per room. Having said that, it is possible to find care facilities with private rooms.

Living conditions in a nursing home are more in line with those a hospital provides. In fact, many seniors who are released from a hospital go to a nursing home for some rehabilitation before they return home.

The care a nursing home resident receives is much more extensive. Nursing home residents have physical therapists who work with them on a daily basis, helping them retain or increase their strength.

A nursing home resident is one who can't be cared for at home, but needs care for a more extensive period of time than a hospital provides. These facilities are geared more for aiding in recovery from an illness or stroke. They cater to patients with dementia and Alzheimer's and are a place for a full-time resident who needs constant care.

HOW TO CHOOSE THE RIGHT NURSING HOME

Those of us who have had to research this matter have found out that not all nursing homes are created equal. They are very diverse. The biggest factor, other than cleanliness and their staff, I have found, is their philosophy regarding their residents.

There are two philosophies. Philosophy #1 – a care facility is a place to warehouse old people. They take medical care of their residents, but keeping the residents stimulated and active is not a concern. This may sound cruel and unjust, but if you have ever visited many homes, you will know that what I'm relaying to you is correct. Their residents sit in their wheelchairs in the halls, listless and uninspired.

Let's call them Home #1 and Home #2. Home #1 doesn't appreciate unexpected visits. When making the initial visit, you must sign up for a tour. On the tour, if you ask to walk around a little and talk to the residents, you will be discouraged from doing so. There is very little stimulation for their residents. The facility is hot, crowded and stinky.

Home #2 takes a different approach. They welcome and encourage the families of their residents to visit at any time. Their residents are clean and their environment is also well kept. There is a trend becoming popular for Home #2 types of nursing homes that would allow their residents to wake up on their own schedule, instead of forced wake-ups, breakfast schedules, and dressing for the day requirements. In other words, waking up on their own schedule and a morning of hanging out in their pajamas is allowed.

They have ample staff who are there to help the residents. They have staff whose main job is to create activities for the residents. Not just activities, but stimulating activities and events. Their residents have things to do and are encouraged to participate in all activities.

When we moved Mom into the nursing home, she was not a happy camper. She didn't want to leave her home, her dog, or her plants. She had lost drastic amounts of weight and was very weak. We took her up to the IVH and admitted her.

One of the first places we took her to, after we had checked her in as a family, was the cafeteria. I was pushing her in a wheelchair and we had just finished eating. One of the people who worked in the cafeteria walked up to Mom and reached out and took her hand. She looked Mom in the eye and said she was so glad to see Mom and was happy she had come to live with them. It made all the difference in the world to her. To this day, I believe that cafeteria worker was an angel!

As you might expect, my parents' care facility is like Home #2. Mom went from being physically weak and a complete shut-in, to joining the IVH choir, going on bus trips with the choir, taking bus trips to go out to eat, and doing ceramics.

Any resident who wishes to, can have a job around the facility. Many people choose to do ceramics and they sell them in the IVH gift shop. Mom's expertise is house plants. Not only does she have them in her room, but she takes care of the ones on her floor. Wow! What a change for her. She actually has a purpose. A reason to get up in the morning. I don't think I have ever seen her so relaxed and happy in all of my adult life!

My parents' care facility is more of a community than a nursing home. The staff at their nursing home work as a team to serve their elderly residents. The staff's attitude is happy, and they love their old people! This home's philosophy is posted on the wall for everyone to see, which is also Philosophy #2: *"You come here to live, not to die."*

As you can see, not all facilities are created equal. Before Dad went to the IVH, he had been in and out of several other nursing homes, after his numerous hospital visits. I saw the good, the bad and the ugly! One of the best resources I have found for evaluating nursing homes is the Medicare website. It has stats and comparisons for over 17,000 nursing homes in the nation that accept Medicare. The website address is: http://www.medicare.gov/nursing/overview.asp

The best approach for picking a nursing facility is to ask around. Many of our friends and family have been in a similar situation. Get their input on different care facilities. While you are getting referrals, don't forget those important advocates, your elder's doctor and other health care professionals, especially if they are geriatric specialists. If you know any ambulance drivers or paramedics, they are a great resource, as they are in every care facility in your area, doing their job. They see the homes at their best and at their worst.

My husband's best friend works for a food brokerage company. It is his job to work with nursing homes' dietitians. He is in every nursing home in the state. He sees their kitchens and the conditions the residents live in. We asked him about the home we were thinking of moving Mom and Dad to. He was very supportive of our choice as he said they were the best in our state! This gave us a feeling of peace in our choice.

Don't forget to check out the care facilities' ratings on the Medicare site. After you have done that, it is best to actually visit the facility. The best time to visit is when they aren't expecting you. That's when you can really tell about their day-to-day activities, cleanliness, and how the staff relates to the residents.

Before you visit, make a written list of questions you want to ask. If you have to arrange a tour visit, be sure to ask to walk around by yourself and talk to some of the residents. If they won't let you, why not? They should allow this. If they don't, I would be suspicious.

A good question to ask is, what is their staff to resident ratio? How many skilled workers to patients do they have? Dad was in a rehabilitation situation with a nursing home and they had one skilled nurse to thirty residents. When I looked it up on the Medicare site, I was not surprised to see a low rating. An optimal ratio should be more like one to ten or fewer.

A biggie for me is to trust my instincts. I have good intuition. If something isn't right, I can feel it. It is important to pay heed to our little voices in our heads!

PRIVATE VERSUS PUBLIC

One factor when looking for a nursing home is public versus private. In the private nursing homes, the ability to pay is a big factor. Because they are private, fee structures can vary. Our neighbors next door are looking to place his father and mother in a care facility. His parents have planned well for their retirement years and have money to work with. They are considering a private nursing home. Each nursing home can have their fees structured differently. Here's an example of a varied payment structure, based on the situation of both parents going into the home at the same time. This not an actual fee structure, only an example:

Payment 1: They can pay up front $46,000 and upon death they would not receive any refund of any kind. When the fee money is exhausted, this nursing home would transfer them to a public nursing home where Title 19 patients would be accepted.

Because they are a private facility, they don't have to take Title 19 patients. Both parents are 91 years old and if they both live four years it would be cost efficient to go this route. It wouldn't matter if their parents lived two months; the money is nonrefundable or used up. There wouldn't be a refund.

Payment 2: They could pay $76,000 up front which would give them several more years, and there would be a partial refund depending on how long they have been in the care facility. There is still the possibility that if the money is exhausted, they could be moved to another facility that would provide Title 19 services.

Payment 3: They pay $100,000 up front, and the funds can never be exhausted. They would never have to move out of the facility, no matter how long they lived. There could be a partial refund depending on the time stayed in the facility before they passed.

The bottom line is: all private facilities will have different fee structures and payment plans. It would be helpful to have your accountant figure out which plan is best for your family situation.

Public facilities, on the other hand, will take Title 19 patients. If your parents are unable to pay, they can be subsidized by the government. Some facilities will need one to two months of payment from your family and then the facility would make the application for the Title 19 program for them.

Keep in mind, each state is different, but they can go back three to five years to recover assets to pay for their care on Title 19. This includes houses, properties, possessions, bank accounts, and investment accounts. Know your state and its requirements.

If your elder is going into a facility in a Title 19 status, they are wards of the state and the state will make the arrangements for which home they will live in. Keep in mind also that each facility only has so many beds available for Title 19 patients.

One way to protect your elder's assets is to purchase in advance a Long Term Care policy. All LTC policies and providers are different. This is a subject to research; consider the companies, the length of time, and the rates.

Like any insurance policy, it has to be purchased before the need arises to use it. The reason to purchase one is to preserve the estate. The extra bonus is that a nursing home will look favorably on your elder's application for admission. They know they will receive payment for a certain length of time before a Title 19 situation happens.

Another benefit for the elder is that their money won't be sucked away to pay for the nursing home. Nursing homes are expensive places to live. Depending on the area of the country the elder lives in, nursing homes can range from $175.00 a day on up. A less expensive home at $175.00 a day figures out to be over $5,400 a month! That equals over $63,000 a year. It isn't difficult to see how most estates couldn't stand up to an extended stay.

Many elders feel that they worked hard all their lives to build up an estate. They would rather their children inherited their estate than to have a nursing home eat it alive. When an elder's estate is gone, a nursing home could transfer the elder to another home with an open Title 19 bed. No choices there for the elder or family.

Someone might balk at paying an LTC policy premium per month. This is when it's important to put the pen and paper to it. Most premiums per month end up being what a person would pay per day in a nursing home. The average elder stays in a care facility between two and four years before passing. One year's worth of premiums might not add up to one month of out-of-pocket cost in a nursing home. Policy premiums are figured by amount per day they will pay out, age of elder when purchasing the policy, and length of time of coverage. Many older people find the peace of mind reassuring.

INFORMATION NEEDED

Okay, you've picked the right home for your loved one. Now what do you need to have to get your loved one into the home?

Keep in mind, each situation may be different. I can only relay to you what we needed to have. Because both of my parents had dementia, we had invoked the Power of Attorney. You may or may not need to do the same.

1. Copies of all Power of Attorney documents (financial and health care)
2. Social Security Benefit Statement for each person entering nursing home.
3. Living Will
4. Honorable Discharge from military (if going into a Veterans Home)
5. Marriage Certificate (my parents were going in together)
6. Life Insurance Policy information and copies of policy (Cash Value Policy is considered an asset)
7. Grave site ownership and copy of deed for burial plots
8. Application to enter nursing home (provided by nursing home)
9. Complete physical and history dated within 3 months of receipt of application

10. Personal functional assessment (we needed to invoke Power of Attorney)
11. Copy of Birth Certificate
12. Financial forms and supporting verification of all income and assets
13. Copy of prepaid burial if applicable
14. Copies of Medicare, Medicare Part D and any other health insurance cards
15. Copy of nursing home insurance policy or long term care insurance policy
16. Copy of Social Security Card
17. Previous two months of checking account statements

Our situation wasn't the norm. Because of my Mother's combative nature and the severity of her dementia, we had to prove her dementia to enact the POA document.

Every situation is different and may need more than what is listed above, or less. It depends on your state and the nursing home requirements.

WHAT TO TAKE TO THE NURSING HOME

Most nursing homes are limited as to the space each resident can have. When we are moving an elder into one, we will need to keep this in mind. Here are a few suggestions on what to take:

1. Television (some nursing homes provide these for residents, some don't)

2. At least 7 pairs of underwear, socks, shirts, pants, hankies, etc. Most nursing homes only do laundry once a week. Make sure their names are written in their clothing.

3. Some personal items such as pictures. My parents have a shadow box in the hall outside their room where they can put pictures of their families. Mom brought a couple of her large pictures from home for her wall. It makes her room look more like her home.

4. Some nursing homes will allow them to bring a recliner of their own. The home my parents are in only allows leather recliners, because they are easy to clean up if there is an accident.

5. Mom was able to bring a few house plants. Her life has always had house plants. It felt more like home for her to have something to care for.

Most nursing homes won't allow their residents to have pets. This was the most difficult thing for Mom to accept. She had a little dog that meant the world to her. It helps if their little creature that they love so much has a home to go to. Many nursing homes will allow pets to visit in certain areas.

I had planned to take her little dog to see her every time I visited. Mom's dog was so devoted to her. No one else would do. Her little dog ran away shortly after making the new home transition. I tried for over a year to find her, but she never came home. Our Animal Rescue League told me that most little dogs are never turned in. They are usually kept by the ones who find them.

BEING AN ADVOCATE FOR OUR LOVED ONES

Once our loved ones have gone to live at the care facility, our job is not done. We have a new job: being an advocate for our loved one. I can't tell you how scary some people's stories are when it comes to nursing homes.

For instance, my angel sister, who has supported me through everything, has had her brush with a bad care facility. Her mother-in-law was living in one. Her mother-in-law's mind was razor sharp, but her physical body was shot! My sister watched this care facility like a hawk because they would take her mother-in-law down the hall to take a bath, naked, on a stretcher, for all the world to see. This embarrassed her mother-in-law. I can't imagine how horrible it must have been for her.

That may sound extreme, but strange things happen. It is important for mom and dad to have an advocate who have their best interests at heart. The advocate should be willing to stay actively involved in their care.

THE SQUEAKY WHEEL

I know you have probably heard the old expression, "The squeaky wheel gets the grease." Any backyard mechanic knows a constantly squeaking wheel gets on the nerves. Because of the squeaking, it calls attention to itself and when the mechanic gets out his can of WD-40, that wheel will get it first!

It is much the same way with elder care. If we see something we don't want to happen with our parents' care in the nursing home, if we are quiet about it, nothing is done. We need to speak up about what we would like changed.

My sister, when it came to her mother-in-law's care, became the squeaky wheel. She didn't like to hear that her loved one had been paraded up and down the hall naked on the way to the bath. She felt it wasn't a dignified way to deal with her loved one. It took many times of speaking up at evaluation meetings to get it changed.

Most nursing homes have evaluation meetings with family to discuss what is happening with their loved ones at the care facility. I attend them when I can. It is an hour away and if I can't make the drive, I conference with them on the phone.

The IVH has regular evaluations with every resident's family, once every quarter. We sit down and talk with the nurse who is in charge of my parents' care. Each resident has one nurse who oversees their care. I like this because the nursing staff isn't switched around so much that no one takes responsibility for their care.

We also talk with the dietitian, the physical therapist, their social worker, and their recreation person. I get to find out about every aspect of my parents' care. If I have a concern, I am able to voice it. They are very receptive to family feedback.

When my parents went to the IVH, they were sharing a room. Dad's dementia has gotten to the point where he wanders away. Dad, who has always been a shy and reserved person, is engaging in inappropriate sexual behavior, a common trait of advanced dementia. He had to be moved to the dementia floor, which is locked down so the residents don't wander.

When he moved, he received a whole new staff to care for him. When my sister and I went to visit, we found Dad depressed. He desperately missed Mom. When we got home, my husband, being the POA, called the social worker and expressed how we felt. He and the social worker came up with a plan. My parents get to see each other at least three or four times a week and have a nice visit.

Dad is happier. He still misses Mom, but he knows he can see her. In fact, they can see each other any time they want. Because they are so open for feedback from the family, it has been a wonderful experience.

When my parents were preparing to enter the IVH, the staff called and discussed my parents with us. They asked very in-depth questions about them. They really cared to understand them and make them feel at home. Since they have been there, the health of both my parents has improved. Dad hasn't been in and out of hospitals with his congestive heart failure since he has lived at the IVH.

ODD HOUR VISITS

I believe that everyone should be checked up on. Especially if my gut tells me something is not right.

I recommend odd hour visits to the nursing home. Go check them out when staff are not expecting it. If they are upset, consider it a warning sign. Something isn't right. If you are immediate family and they tell you they don't allow visits except at visiting hours, this is against the law.

If they are expecting you, things will be cleaner, and your loved one will be better dressed. It might prove to be an advantage to visit during off-hours to see what things are really like when visitors aren't expected.

Years ago, Mom2 went to visit her uncle, unannounced. She found him walking down the hall still strapped to a potty chair.

ATTENDING CARE MEETINGS

Federal law requires care facilities to do a full assessment of a resident's condition within 14 days of admission, and at least every 12 months after that. This care plan should include measurable objectives and timetables.

Even though our loved one might have just come out of a hospital or another facility, they will have another assessment by the home they are entering.

The care facility where Mom and Dad are residents is not only compliant with the law, but they have meetings about Mom or Dad at least once a quarter. I always attend these meetings in person if at all possible. When I'm unable to attend, I'm able to conference in by telephone with everyone at the meeting, to discuss their care.

I suggest, whenever there is a meeting about your loved one, GO! I know this isn't possible every time, but if at all possible, DO IT! Take the time off work or any other obligation and attend the meeting in person. If it's impossible to attend physically, at least attend via conference call. Care givers at these facilities want to see the residents' families actively involved in their care.

It is Federal law; a facility is charged with trying to maintain the resident's condition. Any facility needs to make sure that a person's ability to carry out activities of daily living doesn't deteriorate. Obviously, if this isn't possible because your loved one has a medical condition where their health is deteriorating, decline is unavoidable.

Back in the dark ages of nursing home care, homes were known to do drastic things to make our loved ones comply. For instance, feeding tubes were installed in patients who ate too slowly or not enough. Federal law will not allow this to happen anymore.

Federal law has also changed the way nursing homes are allowed to treat their residents. Just like the situation with Mom2's uncle, patients who have dementia and Alzheimer's can no longer be restrained, unless it is for a medical procedure.

There have been strides made to end the "one doctor fits all" category. Your loved one doesn't have to be seen by the doctor at the facility. They can maintain their relationship with their own doctor. Most facilities provide some kind of shuttle service and attendant to go with your loved one to their doctor's appointment, if you are unable to go.

It is important to be up front with the facility about what you see your role being in your loved one's life.

For more information of this type, check out www. medicare.gov/NHCompare and www.aarp.org/bulletin/ longterm and resources for federal and local law at www. law.cornell.edu.

NOTIFICATION PRACTICES

I have found, since my parents are residing in a care facility, there are choices I can make. One of these choices deals with when I want to be notified of changes in my parent's health. I can choose to be notified of every little thing that happens, not notified at all, or any degree in between.

Remember when I wrote that Dad falls a lot. We chose to be notified if there is a fall that results in an injury. Dad still falls a lot at the Veteran's Home, though not as much as when he was at home. Mostly, it happens on his way to the bathroom in the middle of the night. He has what he refers to as the "rat on me bed" that alerts the staff when he has gotten up out of bed. This isn't, as he thinks, to rat on him for getting out of bed. It is so they can assist him on his way to the bathroom and back. This has helped tremendously to reduce his number of falls.

Because of his falls, he is now decked out with a foam helmet, elbow pads, and knee pads. At first, I was displeased with all of these precautions. I felt as though it was setting him up for ridicule from the other residents.

Then I realized, he isn't the only one who looks like that. It is to keep him safe. It keeps his noggin from further contact with the floor and other hard surfaces.

He is quite the sight to see. He'll come down the hall pushing his walker in what looks like full hockey gear! My husband always tells him that all he needs is a hockey stick. Dad always gets a chuckle out of that comment.

It is a nice option to be able to decide when I want to be notified. I'd been so active in all their care. When they first went to the nursing home, I thought I wanted to be notified for everything. I was wrong! It was stressful enough when they were home, and I had to be there for every little thing. We decided we wanted to be notified if there's a fall that results in an injury, or an illness. It is nice to have the flexibility not to be notified for everything. It has made a lot of difference in my stress levels!

They always let me know if there are any changes in health. Mom, right now, is being treated for bronchitis. They called to tell us she was being put on an antibiotic. They had already run the test, had the diagnosis and were treating her. What a comfort it is for me.

WHEN IS IT TIME FOR HOSPICE?

"Come to the edge.
We might fall.
Come to the edge.
It's too high!
COME TO THE EDGE!
And they came,
and he pushed,
and they flew."

~ Christopher Logue

When we know our elderly loved one has moved into the last phase of life, it may be time for hospice care. Hospice care is determined by the lack of a cure and/or it has been determined by the patient and their family to no longer aggressively treat a disease. Hospice is usually called upon after all options have been pursued. A loved one's passing is getting close; they are within the last six months of their life. Sometimes this is called the "comfort care only" or "palliative care only" stage.

It is difficult for many people to consider dying. Even though we all realize that we will all pass on, it's not a subject we would choose to embrace, especially for our loved ones.

Hospice care was designed to give comfort to patients and their families when the last phase of their life is approaching. In hospice, we can talk with exceptional people who are trained to deal with this every day. They are very loving and helpful people.

Since hospice care is an end of life service, or a "comfort only" status, there are a few rules and regulations to abide with for hospice help.

HOSPICE IN THE HOME

Whether the patient is in hospice care at home, or in hospice care in a nursing home, hospice is considered an end of life service. The first rule of hospice is, since it is an end of life service, they won't aggressively treat a disease. They will only make the patient comfortable.

This doesn't mean that if your loved one gets pneumonia, a bed sore, or any treatable malady, they won't treat it. Quite the contrary. They consider treating these problems as keeping the patient comfortable.

They will place a DNR (do not resuscitate) status on the hospice patient. Should the patient have a cardiac arrest, no resuscitation steps will be taken. Feeding tubes can be taken out. The patient is made comfortable and allowed to pass with dignity.

A friend of ours just went through an in-home hospice experience with his mother, who died of breast cancer. He told us that in their hospice system one of the rules was to post the hospice agreement on the refrigerator in the home.

The family members involved in the decision making and care have signed the hospice agreement. This keeps everyone on the same page. The decision has been made to allow our loved one to cross over in as much dignity as possible, without heroic efforts being made to keep them here with us.

The reason for posting the agreement on the refrigerator is because everyone has a refrigerator. It is a central location for posting information for everyone to see. This is also done in case someone who is not informed about hospice is staying with the patient for a short period of time.

Perhaps the main caregiver has gone to the store, or run an errand, and someone who isn't part of the usual care is there to stay with the hospice patient. They may not be aware of the hospice agreement. If the patient seems to need the services of a hospital, and paramedics are called to the home, the DNR posted there lets the paramedic service know the patient is in a hospice status. The paramedics would not attempt resuscitation. They would call hospice for further instructions and to let hospice know what was going on.

Many hospice patients choose to stay in the home, and can pass away in their home. But if making the patient comfortable is beyond the caregiver's abilities, they can be moved to a hospice home or hospice hospital.

Another way a patient can be moved to a hospice home or hospital, is if both the hospice doctor and the patient's doctor agree that it is not in the patient's best interest to be cared for in the home.

Perhaps there's no one to stay with the patient, or the home situation isn't conducive to proper care. Medicare would pay for the hospice care in the hospice home or hospice hospital in this circumstance.

Hospice care, in a financial sense, is handled much like a hospital stay. If the patient is on Medicare or Medicaid, one of those would be the first to pay. After they have paid their portion, the personal health insurance of the patient would pick up their amount.

If Medicare is involved, they will decide what will be covered. Medicare allows for a caregiver who is taking care of a patient in home hospice to have a week off from caring for the patient.

They realize it can be very stressful to care for a dying loved one. The patient can be moved to a hospice home or hospice hospital for one week while the caregiver has a break.

After the week, the patient can be moved back into the home. They allow this week off every 90 days or so. If you are in this situation, be sure to check with your hospice. They may have their own set of rules.

The loved one who's in hospice care in the home will have a primary nurse, a social worker, and an aide attached to their case. The primary nurse is in charge of all the care. She or he is the "go to person." S/he coordinates with the informal caregivers in the home and with the professional caregivers coming into the home. S/he oversees the medications, and can do some training for the caregivers.

The social worker takes care of the spiritual and financial end of hospice. S/he is the one who does the grief counseling and prepares the loved ones, both patient and family, for the end. S/he helps with the paper work to the insurance companies and Medicare.

The secondary nurse or aide is the professional caregiver who comes in to do the bathing and grooming.

NURSING HOME HOSPICE

If your loved one is in a nursing home and on "comfort only" status, it may be entirely different. Most likely, the family won't be involved in the day-to-day activities of hospice.

The nursing home patient in "comfort only" status will still receive treatment for illnesses that are unrelated to the disease or illness that will be the cause of their death. Illnesses such as pneumonia, bladder infections, bed sores, etc., are treated because it adds to the comfort of the patient (unless the POA of health care or the family says no to those treatments).

A hospice status in the nursing home gives our loved one access to higher dosages of pain medication than would otherwise be administered. Being close to their end of life, the worry about becoming addicted to medication isn't relevant. Comfort is paramount at this time.

It makes me very sad. Dad is now at the last stage of his dementia. There won't be any "getting better" for him.

He's progressing quickly toward the end, and now is the time to administer all the comfort for a dignified death.

My sisters and I have discussed our options. They are few. Dad's mental condition is degenerating quickly. We have decided to move Dad into a "comfort care only" status at the nursing home. We have made the very tough decision to turn off the defibrillator part of his pacemaker. If he goes into cardiac arrest, the nursing home will not try to revive him.

When we were discussing this, the nursing home gave us a little booklet called "Hard Choices for Loving People" by Hank Dunn. Reverend Dunn has been a chaplain in hospice for quite a few years. He has a great deal of experience dealing with patients and families. This little booklet answered all the questions I had, and some I hadn't even thought of. I highly recommend, if your loved one is at this phase of their life, to get this booklet and read it.

Reverend Dunn talks about the three stages of illness as

1. Cure
2. Stabilization of functioning
3. Preparing for a comfortable and dignified death.

For Dad, there is no cure. He is 92 years old and his dementia is pervasive. There is nothing that can be done to stabilize his functioning any longer. All his medical miracles are used up. It is only going to get worse. I love Dad enough that I am willing to let him go. I know what is waiting for him is so much better than his life is right now.

PREPAID BURIAL - YAY OR NAY?

"Death is one of two things... Either it is annihilation, and the dead have no consciousness of anything; or, as we are told, it is really a change: a migration of the soul from one place to another."

~ Socrates

When it comes to prepaid burial plans, there is a lot of differing information. Keep in mind, I'm not insurance licensed nor do I have a law degree. This is a subject that you will need to research to see if it's a correct move for you or your elderly loved one.

Prepaid plans are becoming increasingly popular. AARP estimates that about one in four Americans age 50-plus (20 million people) have paid in advance for funeral services. An aging population is the reason prepaid burial packages are on the rise in popularity. Many people don't want to leave the expense and the planning to their family when they are grieving.

Another reason for the wave of popularity, is that the cost of funerals is rising faster than the normal consumer price index. Prepaid burial plans can be broken down into two basic varieties. The first is a "guaranteed" plan. A funeral home promises that if you pay today's prices, it will provide the same goods and services at today's prices no matter how much prices have increased. The second way is the "non-guaranteed" plan which offers no such protection. But if these accounts appreciate in value, heirs get to keep the gains. This prepayment plan can be done in one lump sum or over time.

The guaranteed plans don't always take care of the unexpected costs. Items such as flowers and music are often left out of the plans. Changes such as casket upgrades or switching to another funeral home can void the price guarantee.

There can be many financial costs and penalties for cashing in these plans. This is an insurance contract and cashing in an insurance policy can be met with a variety of fees and penalties. People who want their cash out of a plan can meet financial resistance. They are entitled to only the cash value (the premiums paid, minus commissions and costs, such as administration costs).

The attraction for buying prepaid plans is that the cost of funerals is skyrocketing. My husband and I saw this at first hand this month. We had a funeral to arrange. The wife of the couple we care for because their sons preceded them in death, passed away in the care facility. Their care facility is in a small town about 30 miles away from where we live.

Two years ago, we bought prepaid burial plans for my parents. When we were interacting with the Iowa Veterans Home, we discovered my parents had some money which the IVH recommended we spend down. Otherwise, the Veterans Home would have no choice but to spend this money for the cost of their care. They suggested we use these funds to buy prepaid burial plans for my parents.

We went to the funeral home we have done business with before, and met with the representative. We purchased two funeral plans, including vaults, caskets, flowers, music, rent for using the facility, obituaries, etc. We didn't purchase the headstone or burial plots in this plan, as we have a family plot already paid for. We spent $10,000 apiece.

Fast forward to this month. When we planned a similar funeral for our friend, we didn't have to pay for the plots; the boys were already buried there. The tombstone was already set in place. The couple has been living at the Masonic Home and the funeral could be held there in their chapel. We didn't have to rent a location to have the funeral.

We were shocked. In the two years since we had paid for my parents' burial insurance plan, the cost had gone up over $2,000!

I have found by doing my research that there are two schools of thought for this purchase. The "yeah" or "two thumbs up" opinion, says this is a smart move because of the ability to lock in the cost of a funeral. It acts like a hedge against inflation in an industry that has steadily climbing costs. It also gives one the ability to plan their own arrangements instead of having their grieving relatives come up with the funeral and the costs of it all.

When people are grieving, it's easy to overspend on a funeral and burial. They feel like this is a reflection of their feelings for the person who has died. I saw this happen after my brother-in-law's death last spring. Bless her heart, my sister-in-law was devastated by her husband's death and only the best would do. This is all right if money is no object. But if we will be spending ourselves into debt to provide an elaborate display, writing the check for that debt every month will only be a gruesome reminder of our extravagance and loss.

Also in the "yeah" camp is the situation we went through with my parents. We needed to spend down their money. Otherwise it would have been spent on their living arrangements and we wouldn't have had anything left at the end for burial. Consumer advocates also claim these plans are most appropriate for people who wish to spend down assets in order to qualify for Medicaid coverage.

Last but not least is the peace of mind it gives the person who has preplanned their funeral. The money is spent on the things the person feels are important. They can have the music they want, the casket that is important to them, etc. They know they aren't foisting what could be perceived in a time of grief as an overwhelming task, onto their loved ones – in addition to the expense their loved ones would have to pay at the time of their death!

In the "nay" or the "thumbs down" corner is the fact that there have been many cases of massive misappropriation of funds. There are several different ways to enter into a prepaid burial plan. One is with the funeral home of your choice, or a financial institution, or a statewide Funeral

Directors Association. The funeral home or institution has the plans and holds the money for the funeral arrangements. There have been many cases of this going wrong.

It isn't easy or inexpensive to get out of these association or financial institution plans. For instance, in Texas consumers forfeit to the funeral director 10% of their prepayments, plus half the earnings. Other states have similar forfeitures and penalties in their state institutions and associations.

This industry has been riddled with scams and frauds. Then there are the funeral homes that have spent the money and when the person dies, there are no funds there. The funeral homes have folded or become insolvent leaving the consumer holding the bag... the empty bag!

Often, a whole life insurance policy is purchased to pay upon the death of the insured, with the funeral home or cemetery as the beneficiary. This is what we did. We purchased a single premium plan to pay out to the funeral home. Where this can go wrong is if monthly payments are being made. In this scenario, the insured can run the risk of paying more for this plan than the funeral actually costs before the payments are stopped.

Watch to make sure you weren't sold a whole life policy only to have it end up being a cheaper product called term insurance. If that is the case, the company could be pocketing the difference. Whole life is much more expensive than term insurance.

Getting out of a life insurance plan can be met with stiff penalties. Life insurance policies are regulated by the laws of the state in which the policy is sold. There are 50 different state insurance departments with different laws. Each insurance provider has to adhere to these state laws.

There are older policies out there that have "redemption clauses" requiring a claim within a certain period of time such as 30 days. But such restrictions are rarely binding and modern life insurance and burial policies generally don't contain this clause.

It's better to know up front what these stiff penalties may be before you are locked into them. For instance, in Iowa there is a ten-day free look period for each policy written. In that time period, the consumer can accept or reject the policy. It's prudent to know what your state's position is on a free look period and then use that time to read over the plan and see if there are any "gotchas" you don't like. If there's something you don't want to live with, don't take the policy. Always practice "buyer beware" thinking.

As a way to avoid the pitfalls, you could open a "joint account" with someone you trust or a "payable on death account" with a bank or brokerage firm. If you want to be sure the money is used for a funeral, set up a trust. Make sure you have control of the money before you pass. After you are gone this money needs to be out of the reach of probate laws, for easy access upon death. These things can be done with your lawyer's help and may cost only a few hundred dollars to do.

Here are some information gathering questions, from the website Funerals: A Consumer Guide (http://www.ftc.gov search bar funerals) to ask before signing up for a prepaid funeral plan:

1. What happens to the money you've prepaid? States have different requirements for these funds.
2. What happens to the interest income on money that is prepaid and put into a trust account?
3. Are you protected if the firm you dealt with goes out of business?
4. Can you cancel the contract and get a full refund if you change your mind?
5. What happens if you move to a different area or die while away from home? Some prepaid plans can be transferred, but with an added cost.

Ask these questions and then do your research. Check out other funeral homes and their plans. Don't forget to tell your family what you've done and where they need to go to find the documentation if you pass before the elder for whom you have set up the funeral plan. Be sure the price is locked in and no additional money will be required.

FAMILY TREASURES

*"The love, kindnesses, and value we have
given authentically to others will be our
remaining treasures at the end of life."*

~Steve Brunkhorst

Treasures, the word itself brings visions of pirates burying their treasure chest where no one can find it. When I think of family treasures, I'm not envisioning pirates. I think of all the loving words spoken to me. The many hours spent together as a family, which nurtured my soul. These kinds of treasures will be preserved as long as we can think back and remember them.

There are also physical treasures, possessions we have kept because they mean something to us. It could be as simple as a note or letter written to us from someone we love, or it could be an antique kept in the family for years, passed down from generation to generation. It is these treasures I wish to bring to mind.

A physical treasure might be the cherished family pet. Sometimes it is very hard for these pets to make the transition to being another person's pet. In the case of Mom's dog, she had eyes and love only for Mom.

When Mom went to the nursing home, I took her dog to the vet to catch up on her shots. I planned to keep her. I reasoned that I could take her to the nursing home to visit Mom. The day after going to the vet, my husband and I went away for the day; the dog was staying home with our daughter. When our own dog, Frank, needed to go outside, she saw her chance to rush the door. She went flying past our daughter as she stooped to hook Frank on his chain.

She took off as fast as her little legs could take her. My daughter chased after her and searched for hours. The long search was on! We tried everything to find her. We visited all the neighbors with a handout that showed her picture and information about her. We drove around for days talking to people and checking for her.

I went to the animal shelters every day for six months. Still no dog! I kept visiting, once a week at this point. I sent a handout to every vet's office and grooming place within 50 miles of our city. We never found her. It broke my heart to tell Mom I had lost her beloved dog. If I could do it over again, I don't know what I could have done differently.

When it comes to physical treasures, our parents and elders are in possession of the family treasures. You know what I mean. Things like antiques, jewelry, and other physical objects our families hold dear.

Every family member has different thoughts about these. Some don't care what happens to their loved one's things. They would rather dump it all, or sell it for the money. They would rather not be bothered with it. Other family members want to preserve the things that have been passed down through the generations. This can become a real brouhaha of family discord. It can become downright ugly at times.

In my family, we sisters got together to go through my parents' belongings. We were fortunate that my parents were in the Veterans system. The Veterans Administration didn't give a lick about my parents' belongings. All they really cared about was the proceeds from the sale of the house. The proceeds will be used for my parents' care at the Veterans Home.

All states are different. In our state, I was glad my parents weren't in the state's system and needing state assistance through Title 19. Our state can be quite ruthless about all belongings being sold for the patient's upkeep. This would have meant that all the antiques, which have been in my family for generations, would have been sold at auction.

When dealing with your loved ones' belongings, it is good to know what your options are. Check out your state's rules, and also the federal rules. The help of a lawyer might be needed.

HOW TO PRESERVE AND DISTIBUTE TREASURES

The definition of treasures is: "Accumulated or stored wealth in the form of money, jewels, or other valuables. Valuable or precious possessions of any kind. One considered especially precious or valuable. To keep or regard as precious; value highly or appreciate. To accumulate and store away, as for future use."

I can't stress enough how important it is to take the long view of our belongings. Since I have gone through three different estates to distribute the treasures, I take a different view of my own.

Pictures are so important to each generation. We love to look back on our happy times of birthdays, graduations, birth, etc. But as time marches on, those memories become lost to the next generation if certain things aren't done to preserve these picture memories. Too many times, the pictures of our ancestors get stored without their names on them. Eventually, after many generations, we don't know who they are. They just become a picture of some dead relative. The pictures can eventually be auctioned off and we can find them adorning the walls of restaurants and bars.

When Dad still had his memories, we would spend a leisurely afternoon going through his pictures and writing down on the back of each one, who the people were. We spent many hours doing this because we enjoyed it. But, alas, there are still so many pictures where the people will remain nameless forever.

At this point, many people would simply throw the pictures away and forget about them. I can't seem to bring myself to do it! My reasoning is, I will keep them for someone else in the family who may have an intense interest in genealogy and will want to put the time into finding out who these people are. It would be a challenging puzzle to solve.

We have a family picture album, which I now keep, that has the pictures of my family for generations. The oldest pictures are so old, I don't know how many "greats" go before the title of grandfather of my ancestor who fought in the Civil War. Dad had carefully written down the names of these relatives. I even have a silhouette of a distant grandfather for whom, thankfully, my great-grandmother had written on the back what his relationship was to her children.

Pictures are treasures, as long as we remember who they are. Here is a thought to ponder. The picture taken today will become obscure to the family in the next 50 years if names and dates aren't recorded on the back. It seems silly for me to be writing down my children's names on the back of their photos, or labeling my grandchildren's pictures. I don't want them to be nameless people 50 years from now. Something to think about....

How many pictures will we lose to the digital age? Many family photos are now stored on DVD disks. Anyone who has movies on reel to reel or VHS knows how quickly the technology moves forward. I have VHS movies of my children when they were little in the 1980s and I don't even own a VHS player anymore! How quickly something can become "old school" and we won't retain the technology to view these pictures. How can we preserve our family's heritage for generations, if it's important to us?

Another family treasure area of concern most people don't think about, or aren't organized enough to have an inventory of, is their jewelry. It slips our mind or doesn't seem important, unless we need it for insurance reasons. Vintage costume jewelry can get passed down in families. My daughter loves and collects vintage jewelry. It will be helpful, as with the pictures, if there is a list of the jewelry and where it came from.

Furniture can have notes stapled on the bottom. The first piece of furniture my parents bought as a married couple was an antique buffet and table. On the bottom, someone had stapled the date it was made and where it came from. When we dispersed and moved my parents' treasures out of their home, we found that bit of information. Anyone who has ever watched "Antique Roadshow" knows that it increases the worth of the antique to know this kind of information.

It is helpful to make a list of where our loved one wants something to go, to whom, and where the item originally came from, if possible. This list should be kept in a safe place. I have already started my "book of treasures." I have a durable notebook that I keep in my antique secretary. All my kids know what the book looks like and what it is for. I encourage them to write in the book what they would like to have when it's time to disperse our treasures. I tell them "first come, first served." I'm always amazed at the things that get written down in the book. Something I wouldn't have thought of as a family treasure is in the book with one of my children's names next to it. It makes me smile! They have important memories attached to these items. Isn't that the making of a treasure?

In some families where there are a lot of high value items such as property, it might be best to set up a legal trust. Another way is to put each item in a codicil in the will. The more it can be in black and white, the less fighting will occur at distribution time. It is really the only way for someone's wishes to be honored. If your loved one is wishing to give something to charity or any other establishment, it is best to have it written in the will.

One thing I discovered, having gone through this process, is that people have different memories of things. To one person, something might be junk that should be thrown away. To another person, that same item has a huge memory factor attached to it.

When it comes to "the junk," or the things no one in the family wants, we tried to think "recycle." Whom could we give it to who could find value or enjoyment? The friend we care for, whom I have mentioned before, had an elaborate collection of "Big Band" music. He had LPs, 8 track tapes, cassette tapes, and CDs... all music from the 1940s and 1950s. He spent time with many of the Big Band leaders. He was friends with Les Brown and many others. We found out that as people forget this era of music, the collections become irrelevant. No one seems to want them anymore. We tried to find buyers for it. No such luck. Finally, we found that many of the albums were appreciated by a friend of our daughter's. He fell in love with the Big Band sound. We gave him one of the many turntables and let him pick out all the albums he wanted. It made him very happy and it honored our friend's wishes to have them go to someone who would treasure them.

REDUCING FAMILY CONFLICT

When it comes time to go through our loved ones' belongings, either because of death or the move to a care facility, it is a difficult time for family members. It can be riddled with conflict. It can cause so much stress, and things can be done and said that can never be taken back. Hard feelings can be crippling to our relationships.

When my sisters, my husband, and I were going through our parents' things to prepare the house for sale, we all got along very well. I was amazed! We were very lucky we didn't want the same things.

The only close call was on the dining room furniture. It was resolved quickly and I don't think there were any hard feelings. It was as pleasurable an experience as one could have when going through two generations' worth of stuff. Keep in mind, my parents were hoarders, so there was lots and lots of stuff.

I know this isn't always the case. When Mom2's second husband died, she was liquidating a lot of things to downsize from a bigger lake home to a two-bedroom apartment. Not only were there many household items, there was a complete workshop of tools. Her husband's hobby was woodworking and he made beautiful furniture.

Nothing was written down and there were hard feelings from one sibling. Hurtful things were said that stressed the relationships. It was not an enjoyable undertaking for anyone, including my husband, who was in the crosshairs from helping out his Mom. The hard feelings have been resolved, but it's never fun going through it.

Many horror stories are made over these kinds of things. One of my best friends, when her parents relocated, experienced such a large amount of family strife. One of the siblings went in and threw away a lot of things that other people wanted. Another sibling burned a lot of the antiques in the yard because he saw no value in them. It was just a lot of old junk to him. My friend was sick about it. She worked a long time on letting her feelings go about the whole stressful experience.

It's a common thing for people to hold on to our physical belongings. We never know when we are going to need something, is the logic we use for keeping all our "stuff." As we get older the "stuff" can get overwhelming. Instead of keeping everything "just in case," what about giving it away to someone who could use it now?

When our kids set up their own households they may not have all the things they need. If we have it, and aren't using it, why not pass it to them now? Why wait until we are sick, old, or dead and our families have to come in and break down our households, transferring the treasures to others? Cutting the invisible thread of our belongings to us can be life-affirming and benefit someone else, leaving us free to enjoy other things.

Advance preparation could make a big difference. I'm hoping my "who gets what book" of our family's treasures will make a difference when it becomes time for them to take care of our treasures. I'm not apprehensive about passing down a family treasure early to someone in my family who might need it or enjoy it.

In my opinion, it's going to be easier to deal with treasure dispersal if we handle it early, not later. If someone has already spoken up for something "in the book of treas-ures," I deal with it now. I don't want to let it wait until I'm gone and feelings are already raw from grief.

I have also learned that nothing should be taken for granted. When death occurs, no one is themselves. Grief is a powerful thing. Feelings can easily become hurt and destroy relationships.

Something as small as a crayon drawing can mean so much to one person and nothing to another. Grief can bring out the worst in some people. It can open up old wounds. Emotions are incredibly high and close to the surface, easily stepped on unintentionally by someone.

In those situations, a Power of Attorney's job can be a high anxiety job. If things aren't done correctly, relation-ships can be irreparably harmed. It helped my husband, when he was the POA for my parents, that we could all get along, and understand each other and each other's needs. He didn't have to play the bad guy!

It is inevitable, someone will have to deal with the family treasures before a household can be disbanded and the property is sold for our elder's care or if they pass away. It would be wonderful if it could be a good experience instead of a life-changing horrible one. Preparation can help. If we want our wishes to be honored, they will need to be in black and white, written down for all to see.

SELLING THE HOME

"A journey of a thousand miles begins with a single step."

~ Chinese Proverb

Preparing your loved one's home for sale begins by identifying the objective. Yes, the objective may be to sell the home, but what is the objective of the proceeds of the sale? Also, who will bear the financial responsibility for the sale of the home?

The proceeds of the sale may be to provide money for the care of our loved one in a nursing home or assisted living facility. Some older people have a great deal of deferred maintenance needing to be done on their home to bring top dollar.

Sometimes, in this case, it isn't advantageous to fix up the home to attempt to receive the highest dollar in the sale, especially if there isn't much money to work with for repairs to the home.

The home repairs money might have to come from the closest relatives, or the sale of the contents, or the elder's money in savings. In the case of relatives putting in the money for repairs, would they receive a return on their investment in the sale of the home? Would it be better to leave the repairs to the new owners and sell the property "as is," lowering the asking price of the home?

In my parents' case, they are in a care facility. They live on a fixed income, which is Social Security. The proceeds from the sale of the house went to the nursing home to provide care for them. When the money from the sale is used up, they will go into a Title 19 status. If they die before the funds from the house are used up, the remainder of the money will be split as their wills designate. It wasn't advantageous for us to find the money or tap the family for repairs to the home. As it turned out, a lovely family with small children bought the home for a great price. They have been fixing it up the way they want it and they will still have some equity in the home. A win/win for everyone. I'm pleased... my family home that I grew up in will have another family to grow up in it and love it!

It may be a different scenario altogether if the proceeds of the home are to be distributed to the beneficiaries of the estate due to death. In that case, it may be desirable to put money into the home if it will be justified by a return for the investment in the sale of the home.

Other variables include, how much work is there to do on the home? Is there any money to work with in the estate to provide the repairs? If repairs are done, will it provide a worthwhile return on the investment? If they aren't done, how will it impact the sale of the house? How much time will it take to make these repairs? Is there a time-line for the sale? Answering these questions will give a good direction on how to proceed.

No matter what direction is called for in the sale of the home, the contents will still need to be dealt with, unless the home is being sold "as is" with the furnishings and contents.

PREPARING FOR MARKET

When preparing a house for the market, there are several things to keep in mind. One question to know the answer to is, are there any liens or commitments on the house?

If our loved one has gone to a care facility, there may be a financial commitment to be honored to the state or federal government. This could be a result of a Title 19 status for their care.

The state or federal government can go back from three to five years on property and content distributions. In other words, they could come back to a relative who had taken possession of the elder's property three to five years earlier, and recoup the property for sale to pay for the elder's care. This could include a valuable antique or any other possession that has a monetary value. It would be best to talk with a lawyer or tax accountant for information regarding these situations.

The proceeds from an estate sale could go to either the state or federal government first to take care of any obligations. There could also be tax and property liens that would need to be taken care of before any proceeds would go to family members.

When preparing the house for sale, how much time do you have? Many people live in different areas of the country and staying in town to clean and clear their parents' house isn't feasible. If this is the case, it may be best to hire a professional. Some professionals will come in and clear and clean for a fee and/or the proceeds from the sale of the contents. Some will take a percentage of the profit on the contents for selling them, but don't do the cleaning of the house.

The best way to locate this type of professional is to seek a referral from antique dealers, realtors, auction companies, or eBay sellers in the same town where your parents' home is located. They are very knowledgeable in their field. They may even wish to come in and look at the antiques in the home and give you an idea of what steps can be taken to clear the contents.

A way to deal with the contents and possibly the real estate is to hire an auctioneer. They are knowledgeable about this subject. They may choose to have the contents brought to their auction house or they could do a tag sale at the home. They would do the advertising for the sale. They usually take 20% of the proceeds.

Our family chose to clear the contents ourselves. Most of the antiques were distributed within the family. In our case, it might not have been profitable for someone to come in to clear and clean without the incentive of the antiques.

When we started the process, we didn't even know that people can be hired to do this. My husband contacted several antique dealers in the area to talk with them about the antiques the family members weren't interested in keeping. They were able to refer us to others.

Some of the people we were referred to sold at flea markets. They were interested in old publications like the *Successful Farmer* issues we had from 1910 – 1945, and other publications. The flea market people tend to buy things they can put a value on and move at a flea market. They know what appeals to people at these venues.

When we were going through the process of clearing, I was surprised at the different things antique dealers were interested in. Everyone seemed to have a specialty. Some were only interested in the antique furniture, some in old publications, some in old postcards and greeting cards.

I was also surprised at how uninterested people were in the old books. All my great-grandma's and my grandma's books were in the home. Both of them had been teachers. Many of the books had publishing dates of the 1880's on up. There were many primers, old textbooks, and old novels.

Old books are practically worthless, unless you find someone who focuses on that particular niche and knows the worth of every book in the marketplace. There was more interest in Mom's newer books on health and spirituality. In the end, we called a charity that has a huge book sale every year as a fund raiser, to come pick them up. The boxes of books filled the entire bed of the volunteer's pickup truck to the brim! We received a charity receipt for them.

Another place that proved to be valuable for selling the home items was Craigslist. This is a helpful site if you know the value of the item you are advertising. It is also a great place to advertise an estate sale. I have heard of great success in liquidating a large number of items in a short period of time. That is, if you don't care how much money you get for the items. It also depends on how aggressively you are willing to price them. It would be similar to garage sale priced items.

Another way to dispose of items is to talk with neighbors of your loved ones. When Mom2 wanted to move back to our city after her second husband passed, my husband was able to sell almost all of the furnishings and other items to neighbors, or those they referred him to. She lived on a lake, and he sold boats, docks, and even the house with the help of the neighbors and a sign in the yard.

It might be beneficial, if you have more time on your hands, to use eBay for selling the furnishings. Keep in mind that you will have to ship the items. It might be more beneficial to find an eBay seller in your area who would be willing to do the work for a percentage of the proceeds.

When we were clearing the house of our good friends whose sons had passed on before them, we called in the services of an auctioneer. Once again, we were dealing with emptying an established household with lots of things. We determined it would be a good idea to use an auctioneer. The only items older family members were interested in were the pictures of family members from long ago.

We thought it would be a good idea to use a local auction company. We didn't have any experience with this kind of service other than going to auctions. We had a horrible experience! Out of this experience I put together a list of questions for anyone who is thinking about contacting an auctioneer for their services. My advice is to interview several auctioneers and go with the one who has the best reputation and will give you the most for the services he offers.

1. Where would they suggest holding the auction? Some auction services will come into the home, clean and box up the items, and take them back to the auction house. Some will want to have the sale at the house. The sale should be close to where your loved one lived. Many neighbors and friends will be interested in attending.

2. How will the auction house display the items? If the items are going to be displayed in the yard, make sure only items that can be rained on are out there, such as glassware.

3. Will they unpack the boxes or just have numerous boxes for people to dig through? Boxing similar items together that don't have a lot of worth may be a good idea, but watch what is going into the boxes.

4. How will they advertise? We were really burned on this one. They told us they would advertise the auction, to be held at the house, in the local shopper newspaper. The neighbors complained to us that they didn't know when the sale was going to be as it hadn't been advertised there. We couldn't find where it had been advertised, and

therefore attendance was small. To add insult to injury, when the proceeds were distributed the auctioneer took out over $800.00 for advertising costs.

5.   What happens to the items that don't sell? The auction house we used just left everything a mess in the house. We had to come back in and not only take the rest of the items to Goodwill, but we had to clean up the mess the auction house made. We have a friend whose mother passed from cancer a couple of years ago. He and his brothers had an auction and it was held at the house. The auction staff cleaned up the items for sale. When the auction was finished, the auction staff packed up the remaining items and per the family's request, took them to the Goodwill. Now that's service! Plus, they left the house picked up and tidy. A house can get pretty messed up with lots of people tramping through, especially on a rainy day. This auction house charged our friends the same percentage as the auction company that did ours. Who got better service? Definitely, not us!

6.   How big a reach does the auction house have? Some auction houses have websites where people can preview the items offered for sale at the auction. They also have a way in which people who live far away can bid on the items, either by phone or sealed bid.

We have an auction house whose auctions we enjoy attending. Their reputation is stellar! They have a fantastic website. The items are cleaned and laid out in advance, and pictures are taken of them. The pictures are uploaded to their website a month in advance so people can peruse the upcoming auction items. They attract people from all over the United States by way of the Internet. During the auction, it isn't uncommon to see one of the auction helpers on the phone with someone far away bidding via phone for certain items.

I love this auction house! They are located in the heart of a soil-rich farming community. The people in this community have been farming for generations. They have lots of antiques that have been in their family for generations. I wish we had been in their area for our auction! We would have gone with them... in a heartbeat!

7.   Does the auction house have a list of happy customers you can contact for a reference? Most reputable auction houses have a list of clients who have been very satisfied with their services. If we had it to do over, I would have contacted their references. If they didn't have any, that would have been a red flag for me.

Experience is a great teacher. I wish I'd known these questions to ask before we had our auction.

A tag sale can be another option some auctioneers provide. There are some companies that only do tag sales. The above list of questions can be modified to help you find the best company for a tag sale. Tag sales are always done in the home. They can be a one- or two-day event. It's a great way to sell antiques, if you know the value of them beforehand. It's important to choose a service that really knows the value of the items in the sale. It's also a great way for people to see the inside of a home which will be on the market soon.

When clearing a home, don't forget local charities. Items can be donated to Salvation Army and Goodwill. There are places such as woman's abuse shelters and organizations that take care of the homeless.

Some places such as the DAV (Disabled American Veterans) or the Salvation Army will come to the house and pick up your items. They are able to take a diversity of items such as clothes, furniture, glassware, and other household things. Food can be donated to the local food pantry.

Even in the most Spartan and well-organized homes, there will be things to throw away. There are waste disposal companies who will bring a dumpster to the home. You can set up a schedule with them on how often and when you want them to pick up the dumpster or empty it. It will be priced according to the frequency of dumping it.

We were lucky in our experience with clearing the junky stuff from our friends' home. The handyman who mowed their lawn, raked their leaves, and did the snow removal in the winter also hauled junk. He was a jack of all trades and his services weren't expensive. He did a great job for us and I would refer him to anyone who wants a quality job done!

Many things can be recycled before, during, and after the project. It's amazing how many boxes can be filled and emptied! We often seemed lost in a sea of paper and paper items. We filled many recycle bins in our quest to clear our parents' home. They had years of correspondence and bills. It seemed to take us the most time going through everything to make sure we didn't recycle an important or valuable item.

The way you choose to clear and clean out your loved one's house should be the one that works best for your temperament, time constraints, and financial considerations. There isn't a right way or a wrong way to do it. It can at times feel overwhelming. I always tried to keep in mind the old saying, "inch by inch, it's a cinch." One bite at a time!

LISTING THE HOME

Once the home has been cleared and cleaned, it is time to find a buyer. This can be an interesting process. Most people will automatically go to a realtor to list it. This is a good idea as realtors are trained professionals who know all the steps to take for a successful home transaction. They will of course receive a fee from the sale of the home.

Some people are more adventuresome. They would rather do the work and keep the commission of the sale of the home as part of the profit.

When my husband sold Mom2's home, he let all the neighbors know the house was going on the market. He let them know early, before he had actually listed the home with a realtor. He was contacted immediately by some friends of the neighbors, who were looking to relocate back to the lake Mom2's home is on. My husband showed them the home.

He had visited with the realtor he wanted to list with. They gave their idea of what the home should sell for. While the people to whom he'd shown the home were "thinking about it," he listed it with the realtor. He put those people on an exclusion list he gave to the realtor. The exclusion list is for people who have seen a home and may be interested in it, before a realtor is called in.

The people decided within a couple of days to go ahead with the purchase. Since my husband wasn't knowledgeable about real estate matters, the realtor handled the transaction and received a decreased commission. Instead of receiving the entire commission for the transaction, the realtor received the amount of commission they would have earned if they had listed it and another realtor had sold it. This paid the realtor for their expertise in the actual closing of the sale. Unless you are a realtor in the state where the home is located, it might be best to proceed with the help of a licensed realtor in that state.

Cleaning, clearing, and listing the family home can seem daunting. Only you and your family know the situation, and can make the proper decisions on how to proceed.

CONCLUSION

"The best portion of a good man's life: his little, nameless, unremembered acts of kindness and love."

~ William Wordsworth

Writing about the world of elder care is a huge undertaking. There is an enormous amount of information out there. As I wrote in the beginning of this book, every one of our older loved ones is different. As different as snowflakes. There isn't a hard and fast rule, one size fits all, for elder care.

My intention in writing this book was to provide information you can use to make your path a little easier. I hope you will see and feel that you aren't alone in your quest to help those you love have an easier time growing older.

I know the road isn't smooth. At times, it is fraught with stress. It isn't easy to care for another person in any phase of life. If they are an infant, they will grow older and become less dependent. But when a person is in their older years it is a whole other endeavor. They will not grow older and need you less, like the infant. They'll grow older and need you more. The roles reverse and the child becomes the parent.

If we can approach this challenge with love and an effort to do our best, the gifts we will receive will far outweigh the adversities we encounter.

Don't be afraid to seek out the information you need to make your journey easier. There's a wonderful community of people who are going through the same things as you. Reach out to them. You will find them online and in your physical location. I hope you will find as I have, that those who deal with the elderly are a loving bunch of folks!

I want to leave you with a thank you. Without you, there wouldn't be a reason for this book. It's been a wonderful thing for me to be able to share the knowledge I have about this subject. Writing this book has taken me down memory lane. I have laughed, shed some tears, and come away feeling blessed to have gone through all of it!

In a way, I feel as though this is an incomplete book. My elder care work isn't done yet. I know that every day I learn more about caring for our older generation and about myself.

Each of the elders I've cared for has been unique. They have had different needs than my parents', as theirs were different from my father-in-law's, as his were from those of my stepfather-in-law. But some things have been alike. We all age differently. I know I am blessed to be able to provide care for all of my beloved elders. I choose to see my care giving as a beautiful gift I can give to the elders in my life.

One thought-provoking question which has popped into my mind is, what will my aging be like? Have you thought about it too? Both of my parents are experiencing long lives, but colored by dementia. Is how we experience our old age dictated by our genes? Whoever we are, are we destined to experience the winter of our lives like our parents and grandparents?

When we are actively involved in elder care giving, it's easy to look at what is happening to them and feel like it's only a matter of time before we will be in the same position.

I choose to believe I will have control of my senior years. Just because there is a family history of something, doesn't mean it will happen to me. I also know that what I focus on grows. If I choose to focus on their fate as an inevitability for my golden years... it will be so.

I believe there are so many things I can do to change the genetic path I walk. Most of it is between my ears in the way I think and react to things. I can also eat better, exercise more, make solid financial and end-of-life directives for my old age, and keep stimulating my brain. What we think and do will be a self-fulfilling prophecy of our life.

I believe it's important to find a role model. Someone who is aging with grace. In my case, I look at my Grandma Bea. She was active and mentally alert until the end. I remember how, when I was growing up, Grandma would often talk about what she loved about growing older. Every day, she reaffirmed the many positive things about being older and counted the many things on her "blessings" list. She focused on the benefits of being older and the things she couldn't have done when she was younger. She didn't whine about her health when she wasn't feeling the best.

The only way we knew she was having some age-related health issues is when she would sign her letters "old aches and pains." It was a far different approach than that of most people, who spend hours rehashing their latest ailment or pain issues.

I choose to celebrate the elders who don't let drawbacks of old age taint their life with preconceived notions. I have a friend who is in her mid-nineties. She may move a little slower and get tired a little easier than she did in her thirties but she still thinks of herself as young and vibrant. I salute her! She is another one of my heroes!

Each of us has a decision to make. Will we shake our fists at the winter of our lives and think of all the things we can no longer do or enjoy? Or do we choose to see the beauty in this stage of our lives? Only you can answer these questions.

Good luck on your odyssey of elder care. I pray that it will enrich your life as it has mine.

RECOMMENDED RESOURCES

Reference: Caregiver Statistics: http://www.caregiver.org/caregiver/jsp/print_friendly.jsp?nodeid=439

Reference: List of warning signs: http://tenderlovingeldercare.com/holidays-with-your-aging-parents-dont-miss-these-warning-signs

Reference: Website for Federal Benefits for Veterans and Dependents Book: http://www1.va.gov/opa/publications/benefits_book.asp Veteran information on this site

Reference: Consumer Reports 10 Questions for . . . Michael Thomas, Aging in Place Expert: http://blogs.consumerreports.org/home/2008/11/aging-in-place.html

Reference: Design Collective Group, Michael A. Thomas: http://www.thedesigncollectivegroup.com/i-age/

Reference: great exercises: http://orthoinfo.aaos.org/topic.cfm?topic=A00237#Warm%20Up

Reference: chair yoga: http://www.ehow.com/videos-on_3786_chair-yoga-seniors.html

Reference: gait belts: http://en.wikipedia.org/wiki/Gait_belt

Reference: gait belts at Walmart: http://www.walmart.com/ip/Posey-Gait-Belt-54/10716043

Reference: Phillips Lifeline: http://www.lifelinesys.com/content/home

Reference: Hoyer Lift: http://en.wikipedia.org/wiki/
Patient_lift

Reference: The Hartford – Warning Signs for elder drivers http://www.safedrivingforalifetime.com.

Reference: Taking the Keys Away Modules

http://www.aarp.org/home-garden/transportation/
we_need_to_talk/

Reference: The Hartford – Crash Risk http://hartfordauto.
thehartford.com/Safe-Driving/Car-Safety/Older-Driver-
Safety/crash-risk-assessments.html

Medicare Website: http://www.medicare.gov/

CPAP Mask and Machine: http://en.wikipedia.org/wiki/
CPAP_machine

Symptoms of Dementia:

http://www.aging-parents-and-eldercare.com/Pages/
Age_Dementia_Symptoms.html

Websites for Nursing Home Laws: www.medicare.gov/
NHCompare, www.aarp.org/bulletin/longterm, www.law.
cornell.edu

Book explaining Hospice Care: Hard Choices for Loving
People http://www.hardchoices.com

Made in the USA
San Bernardino, CA
19 November 2013